D0519773

GAVIN

Gavin was born in Birmingham in 1984 to a radio presenter and a retail assistant. To her three older siblings she owes her love of pop and *Back to the Future*. When her ambition of playing football for Aston Villa was jilted, she went on to study literature at the University of Oxford, where she also formed a band called How Can You. Architecturally, Hertford College's Bridge of Sighs had nothing on Birmingham's concrete skyways, prompting a fierce fondness for her home city that later became obsessive.

A writer, musician and academic, Gavin is a founding member of the whole buildagain.org collective, has written widely on subjects including Samuel Beckett, Buster Keaton, and Brutalism, and has been a contributor to zines such as *The Modernist* and *All That is Common*. After a period in Berlin, she currently teaches literature and film at the University of Sussex, and plays piano and guitar in a band called Textual.

MIDLAND

Honor Gavin

Penned in the Margins
LONDON

PUBLISHED BY PENNED IN THE MARGINS
Toynbee Studios, 28 Commercial Street, London E1 6AB
www.pennedinthemargins.co.uk

All rights reserved
© Honor Gavin 2014

The right of Honor Gavin to be identified as the author of this work has been asserted
by her in accordance with Section 77 of the Copyright, Designs and Patent Act 1988.

This book is in copyright. Subject to statutory exception and to provisions of relevant
collective licensing agreements, no reproduction of any part may take place without
the written permission of Penned in the Margins.

First published 2014

Printed in the United Kingdom by Bell & Bain Ltd.

ISBN
978-1-908058-23-2

This book is sold subject to the condition that it shall not, by way of trade or otherwise,
be lent, re-sold, hired out, or otherwise circulated without the publisher's prior
consent in any form of binding or cover other than that in which it is published and
without a similar condition including this condition being imposed on the subsequent
purchaser.

for

Thomas & James

It's not down in any map. True places never
are.

Herman Melville

~

I have never been very certain as to the value
of tangible links with the past.

Herbert Manzoni

MIDLAND

In the ground there are pins. Here, the ground is held together by pins. In the sandstone ridge the diggers dig through: nails. Tools, but not the ones the workers are using. A thick wire that skewers a corpse and then flaps madly around for America. From sculleries no longer of this world (from shadowy sculleries no longer enterable): ants, tins, spam cans. A chocolate wrapper, torn, scudding the earth. Impossible to tell whether it's been dug up or tossed just now, the wrapper breakdances across the ground but the colour of it is old. The branding is old. Throats, cracking. A pen pointing and the slit nib of it dripping ink onto a piece of foolscap paper. The foolscap describing a circle with a circumference of three point seven five miles in total. Coming into view now above the foolscap: a mass grave of metal skeletons, what the workers call the carcass. This metal grave not straight but bending. Leant over the foolscap: hardcaps and fag fire. The tools the workers are using. Greaseproofed sandwiches, unwrapped as soon as the bell sounded. A beer can with an inch of fizz in it and a way off, its severed ring pull. Another beer can. Another. A coin turning slow revolutions in the troposphere and stamped on it the fizzog of Caesar. Four eyes, anxiously watching.For a bench to sit on, eat greaseproofed sandwiches and snap beer back: a bomb that never has been and never will be detonated. Under foot always: crunched bone shards. A wolfwhistle. Nails capping two spread fingers. The inverse of victory. Throats, cracking. Thigh-flesh, throbbing. A galvanised bucket, swinging. The air it swings through sandy. Tugged buckles.

Jewellery jigging and jewellery buried. Sand everywhere. Sand in joins and in the machinery and in an earhole. And in the sand: crunched bedsteads and gravestones. The carcass becoming a river. The river becoming a road: poured concrete. Slabs, slags, slurry. As if the grey sky has fallen and laid itself out, flat, on the ground. The road now running through sideless buildings: a parlour, with three walls like a room in a movie set. A mantelpiece. Half a bedroom. The road spooling like celluloid. The road running through tins, spam cans, shadowy pantries. The road raised on stilts and thrown over the cut, the canal. The road running through bricks, hinges, cat nip. On the road: motor cars. Inside the cars: coughs, tetchiness, toys. The road running through piss-a-beds, foxgloves, trash dunes. Then a screech and the road crushing a perambulator. Terroreyes. Heartshake. The road running: poured concrete. Across it, that chocolate wrapper breakdancing, its colour the same as the one the sky is now turning: purple, almost claret. Then grey moongob. Brick houses shivering, staring out at each other from cold shoulders. Between them now a hard and fast separation and no possibility of a quick pedal cycle. In their eyes: reflections of television screens. Thumbs. Hot rubber. Two figures stepping into the moongob, their hair green and their necks rusty. A screw. A screw. Red varnished nails, caressing. Red varnished nails, daggering. In the nails: half-moons. Thigh-flesh, throbbing. A slip road. Slipping fingers. Sheets of metal. The road running, curving, working itself into a circle. The road fastforwarding. The road rewinding.

Fastforwarding again. The road like tape in a cassette rewound by being twirled on a biro. The road crackling. The road cracking. The road murdering a perambulator. Heartshake. Under wheel always: toys and interred perambulators. Sand dunes and trash dunes and piss-a-beds poking up from them. Tear ducts. The road forming knots and nodules, aggregations, coiling flyovers. What the road rings now also a nodule: a dollop of matter not of its surroundings. Islands. The kind of constant screaming that eventually just sounds like silence. As if the sky has fallen. Barbed wire fences. Oil puddles. These, the murmuring heartlands. Because of the traffic the temperature rising. The asphalt burning. The world, ending. But then in moongob, the sputter of electric lamplight. Lamplight coming on like dominoes falling. For a circling curve of three point seven five miles in total, electric lamplight. And then on the barbed horizon something emerging: a UFO possibly, or a plane whose confused pilot has mistaken the lit road for an airport runway. A tossed coin that got caught in the stratosphere yonks ago and which is only now falling. A bomber. A bomb. An extraterrestrial. None of these. Instead: the skull of an elephant. The skull of an elephant landing on the road. A small girl emerging, locking it, and walking away from it. The skull of an elephant, cobwebbed. The tusks like the skis on a helicopter. The slit they lead to, the windshield. The skull of an elephant landing and a small girl walking away across concrete. A time machine. The skull of an elephant, silken with cobwebs. And beside it, a pink button hiccuping

in an early sunbeam.

REDEVELOPMENT

B3

In the littery shittiness of a construction site in the regrettably English mid-century Midlands, this is where it begins. Between two churning cement mixers, on a cusp of crunched bricks, is where our young woman now stands. She's damp. Her head is a veritable skip. Bobbed, what old novels would describe as 'plain', she's barely out of the grammar school for girls down the road from Lozells. Lozells is where the shopkeepers astroturf their tabletops and hang up skinny chickens by the chickens' webbed feet. This young woman is as skinny as a skinny chicken herself. For such a whip of a thing, though, her biceps are remarkably pert: they pop out like Pop Eye's from under her overalls' blue sleeves. At night before sleeping she tenses her muscles, taps them, and then, satisfied, nods off, smiling. Her upper-body strength is the one solid thing she considers she has. The clouds make skid-marks in the sky above her. A whoosh of air flips back her fringe.

It's not that she needs the money. That isn't the reason why she's here, now, stood between cement mixers. It's not that she needs money. What would she need money for? She's a young woman. She lives at home still, and home, down the other road from Lozells, so that Lozells was what she crossed on her way everyday to school — home for this young woman has until recently been totally homely, as squeaky as the wheels of a homemade tea trolley. She was good in school to boot. Had she wanted to, she could easily have gone on to university. Or being as she is a woman, she could have gone to the secretarial college, whose buildings she has just now seen being demolished.

Her brain is much brighter than the slump of sky she lives under.

This is why she is here. Two main things.

First, it turned out that she was not begotten by whom she thought: her parents were not her parents. Second, she became the unbeloved of a young man who called himself Zero. After these two things became cumulative, this young woman came to the point where the best she could do was think of herself as an empty crisp packet adrift in a puddle. Or as a beer can's snapped and abandoned ring-pull. That at least was how she put her situation to herself in the pages of her inevitable diary. To begin with she cried a bit. Tears sat fatly in her dimples. The tips of her fingers gave off precisely quantified shivers. But very quickly she realised that the only thing for it was to embrace the grimness, inhabit it, and so off she went to get herself some work on this construction site.

That is the short if not the long of it.

Sometimes this young woman forgets she is *such* a young woman.

Sometimes this young woman forgets she is a young woman.

Her muscles are becoming more muscly. Her palms have stopped shivering and are rapidly toughening. There is something about the neck of a crane and the hook that hangs from it that she finds compelling, calming yet portentous. The thrill that comes from being wolf-whistled whilst wearing oversized overalls and cooking concrete — that too has something to do with why she's standing here, now, stamping rocks into gravel, her eyes stinging from the grit.

The dust rolls towards her in giant mothballs from the space where the secretarial college was. She coughs.

In all seriousness: this young woman here considers herself a teleported *Trümmerfrau*. She reckons herself a rubble woman transported from smashed Berlin, a city to which she's never been, to this shoddy city here, a city which also happens to have a name that begins with a 'b', a name that in certain circles and industries means *counterfeit, cheap, showy*. Used as an adjective, the name of this city of hers turns something valuable into something bogus. Apart from bogusness, however, words such as *cheap* and *showy* don't much match with what our young woman now sees before her, because what she sees now before her is many crumpled walls in her immediate vicinity, a wrecking ball in the middle of everything, and in the distance a bleary mess of disgusting Victorian buildings. Either side of her like nauseous stomachs the cement mixers churn. The sky lurches. Everything around her is literally rubbish. This city is not Berlin and this young woman here is only a *Trümmerfrau* in her crummy *Traüme*.

She breathes.

After grammar school was over, one of her classmates went to work in a village in southern Africa. To our young woman that option seemed more a cop-out than it was laudable. To remain amongst the crisp packets and puddles — to *be* a crisp packet in a puddle, watching as the wrecking balls wrought their pendulous damage on a place that's a wreck already anyroad — staying put, to her way of thinking, was the better endeavour. To stay put was heroic in its foregoing of heroism. It was inconsequential. It was a thorough plunge into *thoughtlessness*, a word she and Zero had had many debates about. Legging it to Africa may have been what that French poet with a name pronounced 'Rambo' had done, but staying put as a misplaced *Trümmerfrau* was better.

So here she is, stood in a dump. Call her Stig.

Back when she herself was shoddily begotten, the wrecking balls were bombs, like they were in Berlin.

All before her lies an expanse of littered listlessness. Amongst the aghast and battered, amongst those who have never *geträumt* a crummy *Traum*, amongst those who can't even boast of a German O-Level — in this city that begins with a 'b', is where she will be.

On her big toe rests the plate of a spade. Beneath the toe rests the skeleton of an old road, and the carcass of a new one.

But the thing is, there's also this: there's still a bit of this skinny strong smart stubborn young woman that wishes she wasn't here. To that itch she has to admit. There's a bit of her that would rather not be another pained fizzog traipsing home along acorned pavements, all be her a pained fizzog who spends her days decked out in overalls, poised between cement mixers, eclipsed by great cranes. The tiny but shiny difference between remaining here in this shoddy city out of laziness or wastedness and staying here in a state of blessedness because of a decision — that difference can be difficult to see. Zero, in his way, did his best to point out this out to her. He tried. It's true. And what Zero said to this bold burly bobbed young woman when eventually he gave up on her, shrugged, and alone went away — what he said to her then is what now prods at her as she stands in the littery shittiness of a construction site in the regrettably English mid-century Midlands:

"Yower out of time, bab."

PRECIPITATION

B3

In the cemetery, which is the heart of me, there is a bab, squat, pissing. It is dark, like. The piss fizzes. The bab hiccups. There is another throat hiccupping near her. This other throat gargles the dark, goes:

"Urroy up!"

The piss fizz foams. The bab's petticoat tickles the turf. The cathedral's stones slowly churn. The stained-glass windows have none of their colours now. In the glass eye of a horrified shepherd I could engineer a twinkle, but I don't: no one would notice I if did, so I don't. The deep soft stone hums. I too hum. I rattle, I whir. I, this grotty, carbuncular city, am dull because of the dead air, because all my facades are tarry with machine-sweat and the flatulence of foundries. I am filthy. I have been becoming filthier and filthier for over a century now. First it began as a gentle chug, a slow, industrious grunge. Then it became heavier. Then it never stopped.

If seen from above, e.g. by a pigeon, or else by a bomb, the cemetery the bab is pissing in takes the shape of a trapezoid. There are two main arteries that suck on it: Temple Road on the one side and on the other, Colmore Row. There is also a small, barely used passage. This wiggles its way down the hill to New Street and is called Needless Alley. No joke. Look it up.

The pissing bab absently laughs. Her urine rushes into the thinning grass. This bab here has removed her knickers: so as to avoid pissing on them, she has taken them all the way off. Through the holes in the knickers' frills, pass ants.

The *other* throat chunters something, then groans: "Aw, urroy *oop*, bab!"

The bab laughs again carelessly, carries on pissing. Her piss is perhaps the longest piss ever to grace the diminutive grave of

Margaretta Stocker, Pianist,
who departed this Life in [illeg.]
the smallest Woman ever in this Kingdom
possessed with every Accomplishment
only 33 inches high.

It's too dark for the bab to see what she is pissing on, but I know it by heart. The grave the bab is pissing on is little more than a stony stub, I'll give her that, plus its inscription has been eroded by the fart breath that daily circulates, the wheeze of me, the muck. The words have become smudges, hardly grazing the stone. There is also the fact that, for balance, the bab has her hand grabbed around the bit of the inscription that marks the midget musician's

Memory

so that all

Memory of

the midget is more strangled and more obscured than it would be anyroad.

The moons in the bab's fingernails are more beautiful than the moon itself.

From the direction of the other throat comes a rustling, then a thud, then another groan. The bab's urine stream grows more powerful each time she laughs.

I would bet that this bab has never noticed poor dead Margaretta's grave even in daylight, despite crossing this heart of mine regularly on her way to catch a tram home from the stop on Colmore Row. Home being, for this particular bab, the boarding house her parents run, a tall brick terrace on Armoury Road, Lozells.

I know much more than I let on. I know it all by heart.

The bab's nail-polish gets chipped on the midget musician's stone.

To the right of the bab, closer to the cathedral's entrance porch, stands a statue of the Bishop Charles Gore. A vagabond is hugging him. The vagabond wears i) a pair of slacks, with the right leg longer than the left leg because the hem of the right leg has collapsed; and ii) his hair immaculately gelled. The bab has not noticed the vagabond. The vagabond has not noticed the bab.

The vagabond dreams of defecating, but then dreams better of it. Thanks be to the Bishop Charles Gore.

The bab has just inserted one wiggling digit into her nostril.

The vagabond's dream presently features a tall, rotund tower and, at the top of it, people queuing up to have enemas.

The bab's urine continues to surge.

The bab is the first person to touch the midget's gravestone in months.

In the meantime the bab yawns.

Time — for the time being — is still alive in these parts. Time can still be categorised, countenanced, zoned. It ticks on through the mud and scum, the puff and trawl. It is one hundred years since the midget's truncated yet expert body was buried here in this cemetery beneath the bumcheeks of this pissing bab and, according to all the banners they have hung across my roads, passages, and hoary canals, exactly

ONE HUNDRED YEARS!

since I, this city, was what they call *incorporated*, which is to say it is one hundred years since I, as a place, was combined, condensed and toasted by a table of paunched industrialists, their coat-tails all daubed with grunge, their pockets weighted with the metal they made from their 'toys', meaning small metal objects of various kinds, e.g. pincers and pen nibs. Except of course the industrialists did not actually make the metal themselves. Except also that some of them traded not in toys, but wire and guns.

It's my birthday.

It's a whole century since I became I, since I became a fully-fledged thing to be administered, visited, commented upon and lived in. My incorporation is what they're celebrating in the ballroom of the Grand Hotel right now. The bab and this *other* of hers have raised many cups of punch to me, and now their bladders need to piss the punch out.

"Get a jerk on, bab!"

Incorporation is what gave me a voice, of a sort. There were those who said what it really meant was

REPRESENTATION

but it was only the men who were allowed to vote for my

REPRESENTATIVE

and then only men of the wealthier kind. The babs didn't even get a peep in. It's debatable as to whether I have ever been represented at all. I suppose some would call me a setting, though not much has ever been set in me. I have chimney-tops for nostrils and oil puddles for eyes.

The bab yawns again, then finishes pissing. For men

who need to *go* there are iron urinals strategically located around town. For women, there are gravestones.

"Yo all done?"

It's the *other* one, come nearer. The bab is stroking the grass, searching for her knickers. I could tilt myself and slip them within reach of her trim fingernails, but I don't.

"Ar."

"I saw yo."

"In the dark?"

The bab's knickers sneak into her hand.

"No, I saw yo inside. Dancing."

"Oh. Well"

"I saw yo dancing with Manzino."

There's a sudden swell of sound. It comes from the party in the Grand, across the road from the cemetery. The bab and the *other* swing their heads towards the swelling. There's a smear of light on the bab's shoulder now, as well. It comes from I don't know where – the watch of a waltzing alderman, perhaps. Along both Colmore Row and Temple Road, the electric streetlights are not turned on. The old gas lamps along Needless Alley are never lit now, anyroad. No one ever goes down Needless Alley, so there's no point.

"Manzoni?"

Her pants back up about her pelvis and her petticoat straightened and smoothed, the bab starts stepping tentatively towards the cemetery gates. Her stiletto heels make my heart hurt. The *other* keeps close to her side. Her step is too slow for his height, so his body twists awkwardly as he walks. Then abruptly he stops, snuffs out a sneeze with a handkerchief yanked from a pocket, wags a finger at the bab's back.

"It's not Manzoni. It's *Manzino*, yo dope."

Cemetery, centenary. In the darkness what's the difference?

The bab turns, wobbles, rests her right hand on a bulky tomb.

"Oh, I *did* dance with him, didn't I?"

"Ar, yo did dance with him, didn't yo? About ten minutes ago. He's got a nerve."

"A nerve?"

"..."

The bab and the *other* are out of the cemetery now. There's enough seepage from the Grand's windows to paint them both a weary yellow.

'Ar —'

The bab says this mockingly: she doesn't speak the same as the *other* usually. Her intonation doesn't gravitate down. Her sentences remain pert.

" — and yo've got a fizzog as long as Livery Street!"

It's not a phrase that the bab uses often, obviously.

"Then walk down it with me."

The bab's eyebrow involuntarily flinches.

"What?"

The *other*, his fizzog as chiseled as the bab's lovely back, stares at her soberly, strongly. Livery Street is very near to the cemetery. It sinks down from the segment of Colmore Row that overreaches the cemetery. Livery Street is as long as a sad fizzog, a sad face, if it's really necessary to spell it out.

"Or stand at the top of it with me. Come on. Yo can fit big distances between a thumb and a finger, yo know."

"What?"

The *other* smiles.

"Come on."

Gently, ever so carefully, the *other* moves his hand to the shallow of the bab's back. From there he can get a feel of her bumcheeks. I think of bringing the kerb up to deck the *other*, but don't.

"Come on."

"Nah, can't. I'm zonked."

"Aw, come on. I'll show yo what he wants to do, what he's got planned, like."

"What who wants to do, you daft young man?"

"Manzino, who else? But don't say that."

"Don't say what?"

"That I'm daft and young. Don't."

Into the dimness now hisses a blister of fire. The bab has lit up. She sucks on the cigarette steadily, and when she takes it out it goes *pop*.

"Nah, it's me that's an old dreary fool. A dreary old deary at twenty!"

"Never."

This whisper wins the *other* a quick but fond glance

from the bab. From the Grand now comes another swell of sound: this time a piano can be made out. The notes zigzag and crash. Voices zigzag and crash too. Outside, the bab and the *other* remain stupidly rooted to the ground. In front of them the Grand stands stupidly too, its gaudy Victorian ornamentation giving the impression of an oversized babba decked out in fancy clothes.

"I've never really liked balls."

That's the bab. But then why did she say to her mom that she *so* wanted to come?

"I've never liked the Grand."

That's the *other*. The bab turns to him, curious. Her ears, which are very small, wiggle.

"But everybody likes the Grand."

"Not me, bab. It's prissy. Fussy. All over the place. Look at all those frills. And inside it's like wading through a gobbed-up piece of marblecake."

The bab sucks deeply on the cigarette, holding onto it between two fingers. If the *other* were smoking a cigarette, it would be held between a finger and a thumb.

"I suppose so. I've never much liked marblecake."

The *other* shakes his head at her.

"Me neither, bab."

" ..."

" ..."

"Can stone be frilly?"

"It can fret awfully, too."

The bab shoves the *other* playfully. The *other* grimaces.

"And what about what Manzino's going to do, whatever that is. Will you like that?"

The *other* swallows. His Adam's apple jolts in his throat. The rumble coming from the Grand softens, stills. The *other* curtly nods.

"I hope they pull the Grand down."

The bab meanwhile pulls a fizzog of mock-horror.

"But they won't."

They won't. I know they won't. With its glittery ballrooms and gyratory staircases, the Grand is glamour, excitement and dances, civic parties and centenary balls. The Grand is ladies in gowns and well-dressed gentlemen gyrating up and down the gyratory staircases. The Grand is chandeliers prettily tinking and beneath them, elderly alderman unprettily twisting. The Grand is bunting and trumpets, pumping. Exhausted punchbowls. Froth. The awful boredom of being so amused. In spite of myself, I hope that the bab goes along with the *other* to Livery Street, or else that she returns to the midget's gravestone and lies herself calmly down. In her very own pool. It would be beautiful, I know.

To the rear of the bab and the *other*, on the other side of the tall iron railings, the abandoned cemetery throbs. Inside it sinks my heart.

"Go on then, crash the ash."

It means pass me the fag.

"Nah!"

"Go on!"

They grin at each other suddenly: he cheerfully, she grimly. From inside the Grand comes the nauseous sound of many chairlegs scraping the floor.

"It'll be the speeches soon."

"Manzino's. Yo won't want to miss that!"

The bab hasn't passed the *other* the fag, but then the *other*'s not interested in that now. He's off.

"Ar, Humphrey B. Manzino will be wanting to tell everyone about Humphrey B. Manzino's great plan. Humphrey B. Manzino's bosting visions of our humble town!"

'We're a city these days, you know. And you mean vision in the singular, I think. What's the 'b' for?'

The bab taps the fag so that the fag ash gets on her clothes. She blinks quickly, mutters —

"Gosh"

— and at long last holds the fag out for the *other* to have. But the *other* is not after it now. The *other*, not customarily one for speeches himself, is uncharacteristically but irreparably off.

"Ar, Humphrey B. Manzino's visions of buildings all surrounded by roads, but not nice neat straight thin roads, nope! Fat roads! Double roads! Triple roads! Roads that go in circles. This all here will be ringed by a *ring* road, bab. Manzino wants to build a road that whirls, a road that curves. Outer circle, middle circle, inner circle. The missing loop. He's not thinking of roads as we know it. He doesn't want to build a better road to get you straight home quick to yower mom, bab. He's not thinking straight at all. He wants a road that'll go round and round, ringa ringa posies, we all fall down. He's marrying himself to this town and squeezing a band of hot sizzling silver round its finger! Goodbye Pombal, Cerdà! Farewell Baron Haussmann! It's Manzino's go now! He's going to lasso all this, bab. Like a cowboy. Collar it. He's a visionary, ar, but, wow. He's going to bulldoze right through this to make room for his loopy loop. I can show yo. He's going to cut through your lovely Livery Street — what a mess that's going to make of all the sad fizzogs around! His plan — his plan for our great manufacturing town is to manufacture a town for *machines* to live in, not a machine for us to live in! *Yam-pi!* That's damn good! He's going to lasso all this and—"

He breathes.

"— and it's all for the sake of his friends at the Auto Club. They're the ones that'll pay for his statue, anyroad."

"You mean 'company', not 'club'. I thought all the planners ever wanted to do was clear up the back-to-backs."

The bab hitches her skirt up and thumps her bum on the ground. The paving stones blush. The bab's eyes rest first upon a dimple in the road's asphalt, and then, when her hand goes out to catch a droplet of rain, roll heavenwards. The air is beginning to suppurate. The Grand remains quiet.

"Company, then. This Manzino of ours isn't really a planner. He's an engineer at heart. The slums are a worthy excuse, bab. They *think* they already covered that last century, when they cut through the Gullet and Cherry Orchards to make Corporation Street, or in other words when Manzoni's predecessors scrubbed out the scum so as to build a street like they'd seen on their trips to Par*eee*. But it's not about Par*eee* now, bab. Nah, it's all about the motorcar now. That's what Manzino and his buddies want. They want for everyone except the scum to be skidding in circles in fancy cars. The rest can get lost, as far as they're concerned. Ringa ringa posies we all fall down!"

The *other* collapses, sprawled.

There is a slight frown grazing the bab's brow. The *other* stays sprawled for a second, then gets up, then comes and sits down next to the bab. This time she passes him the cigarette when he puts out his hand. The night is now tinselly with rain. The fag is a tad damp.

"I don't see what all the fuss is about. A new road?"

The *other* winces, takes a drag.

"It's wet."

"It's raining. Anyway, they'll be making jerrycans and helmets soon, not cars. I heard they're going to camouflage the whole factory roof."

"It's pronounced fak-te-roi, bab. And you might as well say *anyroad.* It goes, like."

"What?"

"*Pardon.*"

The bab's frown flourishes. The *other* stands back up. The fag gets flung in the road. I am weary of the cigarette burns I have received from such casual throws. I am weary and wheezy and pissed off in general. I'm filthy. I wet my pants regularly because the drains need clearing out. I stink. I'm ridiculed. I fart, I cough. And yet on all that birthday bunting they've scrawled my motto, the one given to me when I was re-born (incorporated, combined, and so on). It is, oddly, without exclamation,

FORWARD.

Is it a joke?

The bab remains impassive. The *other* regrets tossing the ash. The recently awakened vagabond shambles out from the gates behind them, exquisitely bows to them, and is gone.

The gutter glimmers suddenly. It's me, sniffling. It's the undrained remains of a tin of pop.

"Come on, let's go. I'll show yo what that Manzino wants to do."

Let them go. Let them all do to me whatever they want.

REDEVELOPMENT

B3

The man with his great feet on the desk rubs his chin, which is bearded, and stares distantly out the cabin window. The window is small but the man's eyes are spacious: they bulge (like double bedsheets pegged on a washing line and wind-blown).

The most the man says is:

"..."

The ww[1] sitting across from the man shuffles awkwardly on a stool, spreads her legs, slumps her slight but solid torso forwards. First meshing her digits together, she then turns them, still meshed, over. A zigzag cracks down the valley her hands now form. Grotty under the nails, her thumbs poke up at the cabin's ceiling. The ceiling is cobwebbed.

"I can work *well*."

Still, the most the man says is:

"..."

"Hey, women worked during the bombs!"

The bearded man with his feet on the desk rubbing his chin staring out of the cabin's small window tuts. He tuts as if what he is tutting at is the effort of tutting. From where the

---

[1] Working Woman.

ww is squatting, the window's view is obscured. To try to see what the man is tutting at, the ww steers her body a fraction forwards. The stool's stumps rise as she moves, then, when she gives up trying to see what it is the man is seeing, fall. The crack the stumps make against the cabin's crude planked floor causes the man's head, at last, to turn towards the ww. Her hair is bluntly bobbed. Unlike most young women her age, she wears not a blouse and pleated skirt precisely the same as those worn by her mom, but i) some overalls that swamp her completely, and ii) a pair of gym pumps. The pumps are the laceless sort. The overalls are gathered to her waist by rope yarn, like a monk's cord. The man surveys these items seriously. His eyes blink each time they move.

"Bombs?"

The ww nods sharply, excited to have got something out of the man with spacious eyes. The ww is all set to say more when from outside the cabin suddenly comes a slow, crunching sound. The ground beneath the man and the ww seems to tense a bit, and then, a second later, slips a bit. The ww, surprised, glances at the man for confirmation of what she thinks has just occurred, but the man says nothing. His question mark still hovers between them (it hovers between them like the spider that has now hoisted itself down on a thread from the ceiling):

"?"

All is quiet.

And then outside the cabin something magnificently

booms. Two seconds more and the boom itself booms. There's a creak. The creak keeps ripping slowly in two till it lets loose a magnificent bang. The bang grabs itself and shakes itself. There's a rattling. The rattle shatters, becomes metallic. Through the small glassless window a spray of grey dust comes surging. The ww snaps her eyes shut instinctively. To their flaps the dust rushes. The ww reopens her eyes. The cabin's surfaces are all covered in a cobwebby coating (to the ww it seems as if the spider has spun a cobweb all over the room).

All is once again quiet.

The cabin, the ww notes, is very basic. In one corner is a rug-strewn daybed. On the pillow rests a teddy. This doesn't *eigentlich* strike the ww as all that bizarre.

The man gets up, walks to the window, tugs a piece of cloth across what is really a mere hole in the wall, strides to a corner, switches on a bulb. The spider, stunned, swims back up its thread to the cabin's ceiling. The ww pales. The bulb's shrill throb has made her feel as if her freckles are sticking out, as if they've become three dimensional: transformed into sticky-out moles.

The man now moves behind the ww's stool. The ww doesn't dare swivel round. The man stands still for a second or so, then moves back towards his desk. His walk is that of a thin man, but his belly, now, is ballooned: even tucked in with a shirt, the ww can tell it overhangs his belt. The ww twiddles her thumbs, tries not to think about what it would be like to have a belly such as his sprawled on top of her.

The ww's own belly overturns.

Arranged on the man's desk are i) a half-full aristotle of whiskey; ii) three ringbinders; iii) a copy of *Fowler's Architects, Builders and Contractors Pocket Book*, which someone (perhaps not the man himself, but perhaps; the ww wouldn't put it past him despite the paunch) has wrapped immaculately in sticky-back plastic, without any blip in the wrapping at all; and iv) a pile of plans. Of various shape and size, some of the plans are drawn on foolscap tracing paper, others are sketched on nobbly cream-coloured paper torn out of a sketchbook, while some others have been properly printed on elephant-sized paper. There really is a size of paper called 'elephant': it measures 28 x 23 inches and the ww easily recognises it. 'Foolscap' is by contrast only 17 x 13.5 inches, 'imperial' is 30 x 22 and 'emperor' is 72 x 48. All this the ww already knows.

The wall behind the man is studded with two pictures, only one of which the ww can make out. It's a photograph taken when work on the construction of the city's new inner ring road first began, about a year ago now. In the photograph's centre, standing alone and bedraggled, is a small brick house. At some point the house has been buttressed with wooden beams that stick out, like false limbs, from its side. On one of the walls these beams support is an advertisement for canned meat: spam. From the world of the advertisement, a cheery woman holds out a tin to a small boy standing by the house, a tatty ball stuffed under his elbow and a gobstopper popping out his gob. The woman is peeling, which makes her cheeriness even weirder: curls of past, overlaid advertisements dangle from her cheeks and her nose. In the distance, about a mile up the hill behind the house, a tall white tower splits open the grouchy clouds.

The ww recognises the tower block, gestures towards it.

"Who took *that?*"

The man doesn't need to look, but he does. He is the kind of man that is polite as and when politeness can help him to unnerve people. That is what the ww thinks.

"That one?"

The ww nods.

"A lecturer in geography."

"At the university?"

"At the university."

"OK."

"How about a drink?"

"What?"

"Whiskey?"

The man's eyes are pointing to the aristotle the ww has already clocked. The ww slaps one skinny hand to her open mouth: she hadn't meant 'what' as in 'what have you got?' She'd meant 'what?' as in 'what are you talking about?'

The man repeats himself:

"Whiskey?"

His eyes work heavily as he speaks: bags clench beneath the spaciousness, and above his eyes, scrunching and unscrunching, are two fat hairy slugs. In the throb of the bulb, the ww can see that, *eigentlich*, the man's eyebrows match his chin: both of the slugs are double slugs, i.e. out of each eyebrow grows another eyebrow, a second eyebrow, of a different colour, more wiry. The ww involuntarily guffaws. The whiskey the man has poured for her (he poured it as if it was pop) has thrilled her tonsils (she's taken a swig) and caused a small explosion in her gut. The ww likes the feeling: she has only ever drunk beer in the past, and once or twice a sip of gin and 'it.' The ww has no idea what the 'it' signifies. This whiskey is better, anyroad. Happily, the ww taps her pumps on the cabin's rough floor.

The man snaps his own drink back in one.

There's an abstract retching sound. A non-human groan. The curtain over the window goes: flap flap flap, flap. The spider, in the middle of spinning its web, goes: frigambob, frigambob.

But all the man does is clear his throat.

"What do you know about construction?"

The ww is ready for this. From the glass in her hand she takes another gulp, swallows, burns, explodes:

"Loads. Well, not *loads*, but...."

The whiskey has stained the ww's cheeks with a permanent blush. This whiskey blush obscures the other blush now rising from her chest to her scalp. The man looks askant at her, one double slug upwards cranked.

"But?"

"I know how to read plans."

The man grunts.

"I learnt from my dad. Well, *eigentlich*, he's not *eigentlich* my dad."

"*Eigentlich?*"

"German for actually. I used to say actually way too much, apparently, so now I say *eigentlich* instead. Great, huh?"

The man grunts again, brushes the air with a breezy hand. The ww can't tell which of these three facts he thinks is irrelevant: her dad not being her dad, her possession of O-Level German, or her ability to read architectural plans.

"I used to help my dad do the colours: brickwork in a plan should be *indian red*, but brickwork in an elevation is *lake, with yellow ochre*. I know all the colour names: *vermilion, prussian blue, hooker's green no. 2*. I know all that kind of stuff."

The ww bows her head conspiratorially, brings her knees together.

"I *do* know."

"..."

"?"

"..."

The ww exhales, suddenly bored.

"It's not as if I want to join the circus or run off to Africa."

The ww is a bit drunk. Gunkily, the man clears his throat.

"If work is what you want...."

The ww throws her hands up, and in doing so sprinkles the cabin liberally with whiskey. Her eyeballs she meanwhile pushes out as far as they'll go.

"Work is what I want."

"Well, there's still the nib factory, you know."

The ww's blush transforms into a red flaring of disgust.

"The *nib* factory?"

"Yes."

"*Nibs?*"

"Yes. Nibs."

"*Nibs?*"

"Nibs."

"But I want to work for you. I want to work here on the new roads. I want to work on *the* new road. I want to help build it. The A4400. Isn't that what it's going to be called? The A4400. The inner ring road. I've read all about it. It's already been started. This is the first chunk of it we're sitting by now. Not that it will be the first chunk when the ring is finished, of course. It won't have a beginning *or* an end when it's done.The paradox is that a circle does have a beginning until the circle is finished but then when the circle is finished it has no finish and no beginning."

"..."

"Are you using concrete or asphalt, or both?"

"..."

"The gist of this is that I'd like to work on the roads. *The* road."

"But you've never worked before."

"So?"

After saying this the ww nosily slurps the last of the whiskey (she slurps it up as she would the last fizz of a tin of pop). A straw would be useful at this point, so the ww looks around for a straw, catches herself, wonders what on earth she is doing with a tumbler of whiskey searching for a straw in a cobwebby cabin with such a useless excuse for a window.

But all the man does is repeat her indolence back to her:

"So."

The ww has been drinking whiskey as if it was pop.

"To borrow a phrase from someone once fond to me, nibs are out of time."

The man smiles.

"They are?"

"Of *course*."

This the ww positively drawls.

"Well."

"Have you not even heard of the biro? No one uses nibs anymore. Well, we had to have a fountain pen in school, but they were such a faff. *Especially* if you're left-handed. At school they tried to force me to write right-handed, because if you write left-handed with a fountain pen then everything always gets smudged. It doesn't matter with a biro. They don't smudge. They don't leave themselves behind themselves, as it were. There's not all that stupidity about changing the nib and sticking it in the ink well and waiting for it suck the ink up. Even if the nibs all together in the nib box do make good maracas, I am *not* going to work in a pen nib factory. No way. Nibs are *out*."

The ww's lower lip pitches forward, yaws, then sulks. The sounds outside the cabin have started to mumble again, but the man does not seem concerned. All he does is ask:

"And what time is now?"

The ww ignores him.

"I want to work on the road. I'm strong. I am. I can beat blokes in an armwrestle."

The ww sticks out an arm from under her overalls. The arm bends into a right angle. Her bicep creases, twitches, then firms. In her hand, the whiskey glass clings bravely on.

"I could armwrestle you."

For the first time in the interview, the man brightens. Then this brand new fizzog of his splits into a rictus, and from the rictus comes a high-pitched giggle. The ww flops her arm, shocked. But the man is all busyness now (the slugs above his big eyes have turned into two wriggling mice). Convulsed, almost dribbling because of the giggles that are pinching the two corners of his mouth (the rictus) he slides towards his belly from out of the desk a flat, green-felted drawer, pauses, convulses again, then picks out a pen. The pen is enameled, expensive, engraved with what might be a name but which doesn't exactly look like one. The first initial is *E*. Then it says *B*, then 3.

At nothing in particular, the ww gasps.

Chuckling still, the man next removes an oblong box, shakes it, places it next to the pen (he put the pen on the desk as if it was a gun).

Then everything is quieter than quiet. Then outside the cabin there's a throttled shout. Then something thuds. The man tuts again, but doesn't glance up from what he is writing. The ww skidded a bit on her stool when there was the thud, but now, while the man is writing, she has returned to flexing her biceps.

From outside the cabin rise voices. The voices are roaring and fraught. The cabin door cracks open so that across the bulb's glow cuts a ray of dust.

"Sir!"

The man at the desk still does not look up.

"Sir."

"In a minute."

"Awoight, sir, but I think yo should come and have a look, sir. Yo see, I think that...."

The man winces.

"Soz. It's just I think that we've hit something."

"Hit something?"

But even now the man does not look up.

"Ar, sir."

"And what is it, could you say, that we have hit?"

"I don't know, sir."

"No?"

"Could be that it's — that it's something very old, like?"

"Like?"

"What's that?"

The man looks up. Now he seems suddenly to have aged, become ancient. The ww swallows a burp.

"You mentioned just then — if I'm not mistaken — that it, whatever *it* is, this thing that you say we have hit, is possibly *very old, like*. Well, very old, *like what*?"

"I don't think I could say, sir."

The man winces again, inhales slowly. For some reason the ww feels like doing an impression of an elephant.

"If you don't know what *it* is that we have, as you say, *hit*, then how could it possibly matter that we have *hit it*? Can you at least tell me that?"

"I don't think I can, sir."

"Then please would you shut the door."

The cabin's wooden door cracks shut. On the other side of it, a voice lurches:

"He says we're to carry on, like!"

The man with spacious eyes (eyes that are also crawling with slugs and mice) slowly blinks, slowly smiles, slowly hands the ww a small white card; sloped writing covers it. The ink isn't smudged at all.

"Well, I think I like you."

The ww stares crazily at the card.

"Come back in a month if you still want to work. That's the address of the office. This one will have changed, you know."

But the ww doesn't get the joke.

"A whole *month*?"

For two seconds or so there's complete dark. Then behind the ww's back the cabin door cracks open again. Against a background of tubes, earth, sand, caps, barrows, gloves, dirt, elbows, tubes, earth, dirt, barrows, cans, puddles, caps, ears, cuffs, zips, gloves, cans, tubes, dirt, cruelness, elbows, anger, earth, sadness, sky, sadness, cloud, tiredness, world — against this background the edge of the man's belly glows.

"As they say, sweat it out."

CONVALESCENCE

B24

I was once a zealous worker. I would go to great lengths to impress my Tis'ers. In my red-checked dress and cotton-white socks, I would pincer my pencil tight and await the wisdoms of middle-aged women with fried eggs for eyes. My own eyes were strabismal. I had a right eye that was, according to one of the slurs bestowed it, lazy. 'Languorous' would have been a better word. I squinted a little, but I didn't need glasses. One eyeball slumped in its socket, but the other was word-perfect with plenty of zip and more than made up for its double's deficiencies.

    I knew I was bright. The others in my class scrambled their spellings and scowled, their eyeballs aligned but none the wiser, while I calmly assembled full marks. I wasn't popular in the playground, but still, the veering courses forced on our pumps by hopscotch chalk and sports pitches really knocked off my socks. I got pretty good at leaping frogs, at walking the moon and dodging bulldogs. As for the less talented amongst us, I couldn't help laughing. Towards other girls especially, I could be cruel. Then in y6 there was an incident in which I was caught hooting — really hooting — at a girl who had fallen over. We had organized a game of and when this girl had tried to cheat the clock with four strides instead of three, the Wolf, who was not me, howled, shot out a claw, and the girl fell over. I was so close I saw her white knickers flash out from under her skirt. I laughed so hard, I started crying. Two minutes later I was found red-fizzoged by a Tis'er, and because the Tis'er thought *I* did it, I was told to stand against the wall.

Worlds End School, on Worlds End Lane, was in an area that had once been known as 'B24.' Up until y6, I and my schoolmates had never known our area by that code. It would never have occurred to us to speak of a place called 'B24.' We may have read it on the sicknotes our parents scrawled and sent us off with, our fists vibrating in the cold, our scuffed lunchboxes bashing our kneecaps. We may have caught the last gasp of its ghost in the bottom corner of some road sign, and we may have heard it whispered under the breath of our grans and granddads. But we never used 'B24' ourselves. Up until y6, to me, to us, it meant nothing. It was there on the few postcards that reached us, but really it referred to nothing. It had no neighbour in any 'B23' or 'B25', as far as I could see, and no connection whatsoever to 'B1' or 'B2.'

'B24' was defunct, a state of being reflected in the state of the place itself. The cats crooned, the pavements drew blood. The roads went nowhere. Worlds End School was housed in a cramped, mean-windowed building that backed onto the cut, the canal. The building had once been a Victorian workhouse, so our Tis'ers threatened us. The exterior walls were muralled with a snot-like substance we assumed to be the work of the local bogeyman.

I stood, once ordered, as close to the snot as I could. The Wolf incident was only the second time I'd been scolded at school, and I was keen to meet my punishment with a redeeming display of diligence even if it meant pressing my nose right up to the bogeyman muck.

I was still standing still when the bell broke up our break.

"Yo can go now."

I had been standing rigid for fifteen minutes and couldn't shift my stiffened feet. I could not complete my punishment, because I could not stop being punished.

"I said yo can go now. Yo'll be late."

The Tis 'er stood immobile, like me, for a moment. Then she shoved my shoulder hard with her palm. I sprinted all the way in to the classroom, shivering with laughter. I was still shivering, wrinkled all over as if the laughter was a bath I had been soaking in, when I sprinted out through the school gates in the mid-afternoon.

I am still thrilled to sniggers when I see a body toppled, when gravity snags balance, when a limb is tipped from its habitual position. It gives me a similar pleasure to sneezing.

I was born with a dislocated hip and a murmuring heart.

The first time I had been properly told off was for writing my name on the Head Tis'er's notice board. This was a while before I became a y6er. At that point, I had only recently learnt to forge my signature out of an awkward hand-dance of jerks and thrusts, and was showing off to another girl who, like me, was sat waiting outside the main office. Worlds End's Head Tis'er had the yolkiest eyes of them all. Her room was more of a sad shop than an office: you never came out of it without a bag of fried eggs of the kind that were edible, the sweet, plasticky sort. Each year she checked our progress with sums and simple reading tests. We were to be well-balanced rather than disciplined was the intention, which was one reason, perhaps, for the thrill I got from a toppled body.

On the occasion of my first telling off I was scheduled to share these tests with a freckly girl half my height. In our boredom, we began a game of chicken, egging each other on to scribble on the blackboard that stood outside the Head Tis'er's room. I would lift the stump of chalk, pause, and peck at the board. She would mime my movements precisely, but with a mark minutely bigger than mine. I soon realised how I could beat her. I let the game go on for a while, but when my moment came I recognised it straight away. I hacked out an R, slashed an I, mis-matched the trunk of a T with its branches but decided to let it stand, and cracked out a dagger of an A:

RITA

I smiled vigorously. I was heroic. The other girl threw herself into her chair like a babba tossed into a dustbin, and our game was done. My signature was my first crime. *RITA*'s sin was my surrender: my eyes seared when she was reprimanded, but in some obscure internal organ — the spleen, or maybe the gallbladder — I was thrilled. *RITA* was doing OK.

By the time I reached y6, my enthusiasm had begun to fade. In spite of my schoolfellows' example, I had not, until then, thought that concentration in class was optional. I displayed all the signs of eagerness, but my eagerness did not come from inside. Up until y6, I had been doing what I thought was ordered, even if the order had never been ordered. I was an enthusiastic worker because I thought I had no choice. It wasn't that my enthusiasm had been forced, or that it disappeared entirely. It was more as if, in y6, something clicked, but not into place.

In the autumnal months of a new school year we wore red t-shirts on top, with crests on our chests to show our heartfelt fidelity to Worlds End, and grey bottoms down below — skirts for girls and shorts for boys. In the holidays before y6 began, I was taken by my mom to the shop where all the school-goers in the world, which was all the school-goers going to Worlds End, got their uniforms. Squeezed between a pharmacy and a stationary store, exceptionally dusty on the inside, the shop seemed to me to be some sort of broom cupboard for unborn children. Instead of the usual t-shirt and pleated skirt, I insisted on being bought a white shirt with slim pink stripes and a red tie with an elastic hook. I saw these items pinned to the bald dolly standing in the corner, and wanted them badly. The shop assistant smirked when she saw me adoringly stroking the wedge of the tie, but my mom was otherwise. My thin-wristed, sharp cheek-boned mom — in that broom cupboard for unborns she was flummoxed but forthcoming. I wore the tie, especially, with pride.

The next week I abandoned it to the dressing-up drawer and wore only the shirt, collar buttoned tight. As I moved through the first weeks of y6, and y6 moved through me, upsetting my stomach and expelling jets of cognitive vomitus, I left the tie to live and die amongst all the other lost properties we kept in the bottom drawer of the chest in the room that was adjacent to mine. The dressing-up drawer was the same drawer my mom said a babba once had slept in. The chest was in the same room my two older brothers stayed in when they were living with us, which was only at weekends. The tie swam and sunk alongside ruffled cuffs and stripy scraps, fake spurs, phony pearls and an ancient peacoat, all the stuff I used to dress myself up with as a natty cowboy, or a sashaying chimney sweep, or an astronaut in high heels, stamping around for humankind.

It was not just my enthusiasm that got lost — but then what it was that had been lost I seemed to have forgotten as soon as I'd lost it. B24, where we lived, was the middle of everything, but it was also the end of the world.

All of a sudden, the days were unsteady and heavier.

Like an obese old woman, the world's walk was now mangled by flab. I stopped jeering obese old women. Time and its inhabitants became more complicated to get along with. It was more difficult to flick a few ticks and tocks off the back of your hand, or to squeeze shampoo onto an ant and magic its broken leg better. I was bored of watching my pet rodent working its waterless mill, wheeling its inoperative wheel, working out — which was a funny thing to call physical education, or P. E., because working out is what you do with maths problems, or problems generally — I was bored of watching my pet rodent working out in its proto-'gym', as gymnasiums and municipal leisure centres were then everywhere becoming. I fed Watt — that was what my pet rodent was called, Watt — nothing but chipshop chips and cheered when at last he died.

"Rita, come here."

My mom spoke the news softly, her head sadly bobbing.

"I think Watt is dead, dear."

"What?"

"Watt is dead."

"Watt is dead?"

"Yes."

"Oh. Are you sure?"

"Yes. Look."

"Oh, yeah. Hurrah!"

It had been my mom who had wanted to give Watt a proper burial. I'd never once seen her touch him during his squeak of a life, but it was she who lifted his dead body from the cage and into its diminutive coffin, which I had eagerly contributed in the shape of an emptied box of Quality Street chocolates. The way my mom took my hand and held onto it after we'd finished the shoveling — teaching me the difference between holding something and holding on to it — this made me regret my earlier cheeriness and pinched from my tearducts the salty droplets that, for poor Watt, had been wanting. His tiny gravestone, a pebble my mom picked up from the path and wedged into the soil, did my head in. I was devastated, but I still didn't really get why. It was as if my mom had passed the sadness onto me by squeezing my hand, except that the sadness had come upon me all distorted.

St. John, who was my father, wasn't there when we dug Watt's grave for him.

Instead of sweating themselves out in the afternoon sun, sadnesses in general started getting stuck in my throat and tickling my larynx whenever I spoke. School seemed absurd. Suddenly, I couldn't understand why I had consented to go for so long. I saw its authority for what it was — an unspoken assumption loosely confirmed in the lawbooks should anyone be bothered to look. I now understood that I had not consented to school. I had just gone, and seeing an action through did not correspond to consenting to it. But at the same time as I understood, I was — as a boy is when first he squirts his spunk, or as a girl when she goes off to do a pee and sees spots of blood in her knickers — baffled.

Baffled.

I know that many people, when they speak, have something they definitely want to tell you. They have the gory details all to hand. The difficulty in my case is that I simply slid into disaffection, to use a word that makes me wonder if what I really want to say is *disinfectant*. I was hazily aware that whatever it was that had gotten into me — "What's gotten *into* you?" everybody kept on asking, as if they suspected I'd been bitten by a rattlesnake, or fitted with a malfunctioning pacemaker — I was even then aware that whatever it was that had gotten into me was not wholly mine, and was therefore endlessly obscure to me. I was even then aware that when moms tell their supermarket-shelf-demolishing-child to stop being such a *pain* there is an edge to what they are saying, a knife-blade like the ones the cutlers made before they switched to making swords. We all begin as labour-pains, and so some of us remain. The midwife washes the muck off but the fact remains that getting born stains both you and the pelvis that pops you, which is why the saints[1] invented the doctrine of original sin: being baptised as an infant gives you a second go at getting the muck off, and also makes sure everybody is watching, which they probably weren't the first time, when the midwife whipped a cold, wet cloth over your shocked little body. The second time around, everybody toasts your spotlessness, gives you trinkets, and goes home comforted. But really the stain

---

[1] Anagram of 'stains': notice.

stays upon you. The labour-pains continue. The day of Watt's funeral I got the first in a series of inexplicable stomach aches, pains that winded me completely but that caused neither me nor my appetite any manifest injury — so that my mom got the thought that what I was really doing was crying 'WOLF!.' It didn't occur to her, and it didn't occur to me, that the two of us were playing a game of Chinese whispers. I didn't have enough information at the time. I wasn't expecting.

There was a name for all of it, I soon discovered: 'the fall.' In y6, the fall was what the Tis'ers were always teaching us about. It was what had happened to my mom and St. John, who was my father. The fall was why my two older brothers, who also happened to be twins, whose mom was not my mom, which as far as I was concerned was just another trick they had up their sleeves — the fall was why my two older brothers didn't always live with us. It was what came between me and my best friend at school, Indy. The fall was why we lived in a world that was obviously ending, a world that was both the centre of everything and totally uncentred. 'B24', with its neat bungalows and tower blocks, its sadshops and postboxes-turned-dustbins, its gardens planted with foxgloves and cat nip, all slid past by a river of concrete. 'B24.'

I am not saying I experienced a major disenchantment. It is true that I still agree with every single book I read and am always surprised to find that the next author disagrees, in whatever way, with the world so carefully assembled by the author who came before them. In this sense, I am still a believer, if a soggy one. Truly, the church I went to was housed in an ex-swimming pool. I don't expect the world to grow from a nub in my stomach. If there is an umbilical cord, then it is spasming fantastically in some shabby maternal ward, housed in a dilapidated manufactory for buttons. I am the lacerated babba, wailing to be tied back up. I am the paroxysmal umbilical cord, the orphaned, elasticated tie. I'm both the baby and the cord. I'm a brain that was born before me. I am both of us at the same time. Let us go then, you and I. Let us go then, RITA and me, me and my spasming bonds, my shimmying loyalties and myself, and let us not stop at Worlds End. Let's get all dressed up and splendorous in those brummagem spurs and trinkets, and let's lose each gem all over again. I'll wear anything. I'll believe everything. If someone tells me the world is a pineapple-turnover cake, I agree. If someone else says it is more like an apple crumble, with the emphasis on the gooey fruit stuff, I can see what they mean. I like to crawl into the corner of their eye and see things from that position. What I can't see is the contradiction. Or rather, I see the contradiction, but the contradiction is precisely what fits the rumbling in my stomach, where that nurturing nub should be.

And so.

~

'The line of the road must obviously avoid
the most valuable property, while advantage
should be taken of sites where buildings have
been destroyed or damaged by bombs.'
Humphrey B. Manzino

~

PRECIPITATION

BI IBB

"Hunters Road."

    "Gravelley Lane."

    "Same. They were after Fort Dunlop, I reckon?"

    "Soho Hill. Miss, can I ploise..."

    "Icknield Street."

    "St Phillip's. Jesus!"

    "Rookery Road."

    "The Aerodrome Factory, Castle Bromwich."

    "Belchers Lane."

    "Ryvita Co. Ltd. The Hughes Biscuit Fakteroi, too. The Hughes Broken Biscuit Fakteroi, that should be. Heh!"

    The bab is in an office in Eden, cartographically engaged. It's a wet morning in early November. The streets outside the office are all sequined with glass shards. These tinkle when the sweeps swoop at them, and make dainty rainbows in the melting rain. If the shards get into your shoes then they are painful.

    Eden is the name of a segment of space that runs between Colmore Row and Edmund Street. It is where the City Council, otherwise known as the 'Corporation', has its offices, and so therefore where the bab, who is these days the personal secretary of Humphrey B. Manzino, who is these days officially titled City Surveyor and Engineer, has her place of work.

The room the bab is sat in is extremely wide: shallow and blank apart from a few framed photographs at one end, but mostly massively wide. It's more like a corridor than a room, but it's not a corridor at all. The desk the bab is sat at is for her a relatively new one. It's long like the room, has gaunt steel legs that keep threatening to sever the bab's own legs, but then a top spread out with fleshy leather that sinks when the bab presses her fingers into it and segues back to flatness slowly, in giraffe time. The giraffe is the bab's favourite animal.[1] If she could, she would put a small model of one on the desktop in front of her and be calmed, whenever she needed to be, by its aura of deceleration. The bab wishes her own legs, which are a bit stumpy, would 'loll' in the way a giraffe's does.

But the desk the bab is sat at is not sized up for any knick-knacks. It has to be kept extremely tidy. Contrary to common expectations of a secretary's desk, there is no typewriter to hammer at and no piles of paper, either. The bab hasn't even dared place a framed photograph of her mom in one of the corners. Instead, spread out across the desk, weighted down at the edges by three paperweights, is the only thing it seems the desk could ever have been made for. A map. The map takes up the best part of the table. It has marks on it like a giraffe does, but apart from that there is nothing similar between them.

---

[1] Elephants are her second favourite.

Giraffes groove smoothly through space, relaxing time. Maps dictate space and, possibly, time.

The three paperweights that keep the map steady are as follows: a pumice stone, a bag of sand, and a single piece of white chalk. Each object was personally contributed by the bab's boss, Humphrey B. Manzino. Each object has, the bab feels certain, some sort of talismanic significance, but what exactly that is she isn't sure. To be honest, she hasn't got a clue.

The bab revolves her shoulders then rubs at the inner corners of her eyes, where the sleep-bogies sleep and where each day's carefully applied eye pencil goes to die. Today the bab has on i) a green, pleated skirt that stops at a point precisely equidistant between her knee and her achilles tendon and ii) a mauve cardigan with matching buttons, some of which are spurting stray threads, while others are sewed neatly. Her hair is gently rollered, which is the way she always wears it: according to the *other* the bab's hair 'undulates.' The way she does her hair is not something the bab thinks much about, but the *other* said he liked it, the way it 'undulated', and so that is how she does it. At night her skull is pillowed with foam sausages. The pins these rollers are held with stick into her dreams and screw them up a bit.

There are only two windows in the room the bab is currently sat in, one high up in the wall at each end. Light otherwise comes from powerful lamps. The building that houses Eden has many broad sash windows, some with marble ledges that are lovely to perch a bum on, but in this particular room there are only two, and no bum can reach their sills. The bab doesn't mind, though, that there's no window for her to gaze through during slow moments. Slow moments come rarely for the bab now anyroad. There's also the fact that windows can be very scary these days, even outright dangerous; stand next to one at the wrong time, and a window can put your eye out.

The bab sighs.

The desk she is sat at happens to be where the *other* himself sat once upon a time. The bab breaks into a smile when she remembers this, but then the smile breaks up into shatteredness: crazy-paved, cracked-cement shatteredness. The *other* is no longer around. The *other*, who after the Corporation's centenary celebrations in the Grand Hotel became the bab's one and only, *her* other, is professionally known in Eden as Surveyor for Area Code B19. The bab misses him badly, Surveyor for Area Code B19/the *other*. She misses his moustache and his vowel sounds especially.

The bab has a tendency to tug at her earlobes without realising it. Her earlobes are unpierced.

The desk the bab shares with the *other*'s absence is one among many. All of them are equally broad, and all of them are arranged in a single row stretched out across the room. The bab is seated to the left of the line's middle, the middle being designated by the great brass-handled door by which the room is entered by the general public (there are other, less opulent entrances, but those are for Corporation employees). The rest of the desks are only ever haphazardly occupied now. This is because the best part of the Corporation's male employees are no longer around.

But there are enough to keep things ticking over.

Surveyor for Area Code B15 still arrives promptly every morning in Eden at 8.59 to stare at his hands, which are curiously unwizened given his grey hair and boggy eyeballs. He eats one spam sandwich at 12.00 and another at 12.45. At 13.30 his work is finished, since nobody comes in anymore to petition his permission to demolish a wall, or pull down a rotting shed, because to do so at the moment would be unfunny and mildly psychotic. The skin on B15's hands, which has lost its elasticity, but which he has a habit of pinching, makes the bab feel awfully squeamish. When the hab feels squeamish she sucks her tummy in and sits upright. As this reflex is good for her posture, B15's pinching is not absolutely a bad thing. That at least is what the bab has decided. Early on in the afternoons, B15 leaves without saying goodbye. The bab always waves him off cheerily.

Surveyor for Area Code B3 still works in this room as well. He usually chooses to sit two desks away from the bab, though every now and then he mixes it up. B3's real name is Ernest, but everyone calls him B3. B3 sweats and festers and occasionally chirrups from morning to midday over the diagrams and graphs and figures Humphrey B. Manzino asks the bab to give him, and in the afternoons he sleeps. In the past his afternoons would have been spent 'out on the district', as were those of B15 and B19 and every other Corporation Surveyor, but these days his afternoons are as a standard sleepy. For the times, B3 is suspiciously young and handsome. The bab is diligent in avoiding his eye.

There are still a few secretaries apart from the bab wandering Eden, but it's mostly just these three using the desks in this room: the bab, B3, and B15. The boss — Manzino — has his own office located off to the side through two doors. The frame of the first door is small, the second one is enormous.

The room the bab works in is called the 'Enquiry Office.' An engraved brass plate next to the public entrance says so. It's called the Enquiry Office because it used to be the place to come to make an enquiry about demolishing a building, or turning a workhouse into a school, but now it's where you come to report a fallen bomb. The Enquiry Office is austerely functional (the best curves in it belong to the bab). The office of Manzino, on the other hand, is suave. It's one of Eden's most beautiful rooms. The bab admires Manzino's grand fireplace but thinking about it makes her furious.

The arrhythmic chiming of Manzino's bell — the bab is still his secretary after all, even if she sits out in the Enquiry Office all day — is by contrast more of a horror to the bab than the bombs. The bombs fall. To begin with they dropped like jaws, astonished at themselves and astonishing, but already they are beginning to integrate themselves into the landscape. The people whose houses the bombs toss blithely aside arrive right here by the bab's desk, some dumbstruck but with gushing gashes that say it all, others with gushing narratives but not a knee-graze or Chinese burn to speak of. It's the bab's task to transform their gasps and pants into perfect circles on her map and, as and when she can, to colour-code her work according to bomb-type and bomb-damage. In addition to her more traditional secretarial duties — duties the bab still has to keep up with, tapping out Manzino's memos and letters on the typewriter she keeps locked in a drawer in her old desk; taking shorthand notes when he's brainstorming a speech — this is what the bab does. The map is her main work.

Inching the pumice stone slighty to one side, the bab settles her eyes on the map. Finding the Hughes Biscuit Fakteroi relatively easily, she points to its position with one digit, selects a pencil with her free hand, stabs the map where her finger is with the pencil. The rest, the detail, she will do when the queue in front of her has died down. The map's key was given to her by Manzino. He emphasised to the bab the importance of making sure everything was clearly categorised, clearly legible to anyone, but he also gave her the freedom to adjust the key's terms. The bab perhaps adjusts them a little too much: she's extremely keen to be accurate, yet it's proving difficult to keep track of her many subtle differentiations, her many careful classifications, sub-classifications and sub-sub-classifications. It's moreover strange the way her colours and circles make the map appear more dense, the city thicker and thicker than it already is, when in truth what her marks indicate are accumulative blasts of emptiness: so many pockets of new nothingness dotted all over the city. It sickens her. It doesn't sicken her. It's a 'bombtastic' job, is what B3 tells her.

'He must be joking?' wrote the *other* in one of his letters home. The bab keeps the *other*'s letters in an old sardine tin in her landlady's pantry. The bab doesn't live in her parents' boarding house anymore.

The first bomb fell back in August. It surprised them all. The bomber had been a straggler, a manic loner, a crazed penguin separated from its herd — or whatever the word is for a plurality of penguins.[2] The plane let go of its load around lunchtime, in shameless daylight, about the time old B15 would have been finishing off his second spam sarnie. The man the bomb smithereened had been a soldier, home on leave. The night before the soldier had been snug in the pub bragging about his battle valour and, prompted by an unaccountable premonitory glow, flogging his childhood drawings of UFOs. The bomb that demolished him had been meant for the rubber

---

[2] The bab, take note, likes zoos, a predilection that has nothing to do with the fact that Manzino once took a group of Eden employees on a 'day trip' to the new Zoological Gardens, designed by a Russian émigré architect whom Manzino kept calling 'Bert' and who really had done a super job, in the bab's opinion, of giving the penguins a wonderful pool. Their concrete ramp was just so *smooth*, and it was such fun to watch the dopey penguins zoom down it on their bums (if penguins have bums). In fact, everything in the penguin enclosure was wonderfully undulous: the rippled edges of the raised platform made the bab think of a fat paint splat, and to the bab fat paint splats are an irrefutable signifier of happiness.

fakteroi round the corner, it was widely supposed. The soldier's UFO drawings weren't very good. Humphrey B. Manzino had presented the bab with the map the very next morning: she had arrived in his office in Eden as usual, expecting, as usual, to plump his cushions and prepare his customary plate of fig rolls, but Manzino had been there already, his elbow resting elegantly yet perilously on the beautiful marble mantelpiece. The map had been there already too, spread out all before them on the Ottoman rug, its lines and contours freshly out-dated by the previous night's bomb, its outline now representing the rudiments of a new world. The bab had said nothing throughout Manzino's instructions. She had not even felt the need to take her beloved shorthand notes.

The fact that she takes quite as much care over her work as she does — sharpening her pencils incessantly, or choosing between a 2B and a 3B with the absorption of an utter perfectionist — does not in itself bother the bab. The thing that bothers her, the thing that really snowcaps her knuckles, is that B3 notices. He notices her industriousness and makes callous jokes about it.

"2B or not 2B? That is the question."

That's a favourite so far. It's really as bad as all that. For all the bab can tell, he has no feeling of sympathy at all for the people who troop through the Enquiry Office door, their eyeballs zapped. He's never once bothered to offer one of them a cup of tea. He's never helped the bab gently to urge the more distressed of them through a tale of total unconditional limb-loss or love-loss. To the bab these wrecked vessels of information are involuntary participants in a perverse game of sudden death. To B3 — and really to Manzino too, though the bab still believes the latter's intentions are essentially good and gentlemanly — the stories the bab records on her map are small steps towards the implementation of a greater system, a greater demolition spree than ever a crazed penguin could dream of.

This is the truth: it's B3 and Humphrey B. Manzino's intention to build on the bombs' destruction. Where the bombs drill holes, there Manzino and B3 plan to build sprucer houses, taller tower blocks, and a brand new road. The bab knows of this and takes pride in her vital role. After all, it's because of Manzino that she's still swanning about here in Eden. She could easily have been transferred to some shadow fakteroi, where instead of making motorcars or metal toys they are now building bombers to bomb the bombers with.

In the fakteroi in Lozells, not far from the bab's parent's boarding house, munitions are being manufactured by women who were previously secretaries.

The bab, as tends to happen each day about mid-morning, sneezes once into her bare palms, pulls the *other*'s handkerchief out from her skirt pocket, and sneezes for the second time. The sneezes are snot-free, because the bab is not inclined to get colds.

The *other*'s handkerchief is initialed not with the letters of the other's name, but with his area code: B19. The sweetness of this triggers the bab to sneeze a third time.

"Gesundheit."

It's B3, showing he cares.

"Thank you."

"Don't mention it."

B3's accent is flat and tuneless, unlike that of the *other*, otherwise known as Surveyor for Area Code B19. It's unlike the bab's own, even. "He's got a quid in his gob," is what the *other* once said of B3. The bab knows that the exquisitely proportioned syllables have to do with where B3 lives: in one of those exquisitely proportioned roads over in B15's zone, where no fakteroi smog has ever dared roam and where, coincidentally, no bomb is yet to venture. There *is* actually a fakteroi in B15, but its product is as sugary as the neatly shrubbed streets and houses, or 'cottages', that surround it. The fakteroi's product is chocolate. The stench it emits is delicious. Half of the bab would love to live in B15, as would anyone who can't resist a bar of 'dairy milk.' The other half considers the chocolate fakteroi and its environs to be an absurdly cosy version of the city proper, a clean and prudish dream inserted into a dirty one. It's possible that this other half of the bab has been influenced by the *other*, but then the *other* doesn't seem to like much of anything as far as the bab can tell. It surely doesn't make sense for him to be against both the suburbs of B15 — their tenderly placed amenities, their quiet islands and village greens, the spacious, servanted house (as the bab imagines it) of B3 himself — and the plans Manzino is proposing, plans whose main material will be mile after mile of concrete — plans that the bab's map is helping Manzino to plot.

"Busy morning?"

It's not as if B3 needs to ask this. The bab's desk has had a solid queue in front of it since 9.15, the time at which the doors of the Enquiry Office swing open every weekday. The queue has done nothing to discourage Manzino's bell from ringing, though, and so the bab has been back and forth between her map work and the business of tea, fig roll, pen nib and ink provision all morning. B15 and B3 have barely lifted a bumcheek. B3 has just been gurgling over his diagrams as usual.

"Yes, very busy!"

The bab regrets the breezy tone of this almost as soon as she finishes speaking. The tops of her stockings are all of a sudden terribly itchy. B3 grins obscenely.

"Can I see?"

He's not supposed to snoop, but he's up and over her shoulder before she can resist him.

"Looks like an onslaught of chicken pox, doesn't it?"

B3 is pointing at an especially inflamed section of the map, where swarms of scarlet spots overlap with clusters of blackheads.

"That's B19."

He means the *other*'s area, not the *other* himself.

"Yes, it is."

"Too bad, too bad! Your family are round there, aren't they?"

He knows very well that Armoury Road, B19 is where the bab's dad and mom run their boarding house. He doesn't know anything about the bab and the *other*, though, or so the bab sincerely hopes.

"But you don't live at home anymore?"

It's true the bab has moved out of the boarding house, but otherwise there is nothing untoward about the bab's current living arrangements, nothing whatsoever.

"I room with a girlfriend — a schoolfriend."

It's not true that the bab's current roommate is a friend from her schooldays.

"Of course."

"Jean. I think you may know her, in fact: she worked here too, but she was moved out to Castle Bromwich, I think."

"Of course. I know the one."

B3 knew Jean rather well at one point. The bab knows all about it.

It comes to the bab's attention that B3's arm has been and is still stretched across the part of her that her dad calls her 'bosom.' But the bab can tell by B3's squint and the tic in his temple that his mind is on nothing but the map in front of them, and she is only too glad to watch his finger leave the red wound that is B19 and make its way back, vaguely but with stealth, towards B3, the city centre. B3, the city centre, is

B3's professional territory and it's in B3 that the first and most crucial curve of Manzino's new road is to be constructed. B3 is responsible for seeing to it that Manzino's plan is carried through. It doesn't much matter to him whether B19, with its lavvies and tunnelbacks, its boozy belches and sudded doorsteps — it doesn't matter to B3 whether B19 is obliterated. He doesn't live there and he doesn't work there, so how could it matter? On the whole it will help B3 if B19 is bulldozed. It will make the future much easier to assemble, and the future he and Manzino have in mind will be much better for everybody, naturally.

"A beautiful loop."

It's unavoidable: the index finger of B3 is caressing the bab's map as if it were her boob. His thumb, on the other hand, is at rest in the city's central cemetery. The bab does not ponder the significance of these positionings.

B3 blows away a fly that has settled in B3, then retreats. The day continues.

"Lawley Street."

Lawley Street's informant is a tall, muscular railway worker with a permanent blush and extravagant eyelashes. His nose contains only one, cavernous nostril. The bab is not frightened. B3's interest is piqued (the bab can tell by the way he throws his feet on the desk and stabs his stare into space) when the man's turn at the front of the queue comes and he drawls, with an especially long first syllable, the location of the bomb that in a single snarl has exterminated his place of work along with a number of his workmates. The informant's account of what has befallen him at no point falters. His one nostril barely quivers. The bab asks the necessary questions, chooses the correct pencils, and then, when she comes to insert the circle on her map, at once understands B3's interest. Opened as a passenger terminal back when the railway was arriving with gusto, Lawley Street Station has for most of its life been a goods depot — and in the last decade or so, a superfluous one. It just so happens to be situated smack bang in the curving line sketched by Manzino as the path to be followed by the first hug of the inner ring road, which will be, he keeps telling the bab, much to her bewilderment,

neither an urban motorway, nor principally a traffic street, nor a shopping thoroughfare.

To the bab this description sounds like a brilliant riddle. If a road isn't a motorway or a traffic street or even a shopping thoroughfare, which presumably means a 'high street', then what could it be? But Humphrey B. Manzino doesn't ever seem to require an answer from her. Humphrey B. Manzino is blue-eyed and gentle. He sleeps in his office, some nights.

B3 chews on his shirt-sleeve as the railway worker recounts, at the bab's request, the extent of the material damage done to Lawley Street. Strangely, the bab finds herself finding his muffled excitement infectious: it's possible she's hardening, becoming more purely geometric in her appreciation of these terrible stories, or it could even be the case — and this is something she'll have to have out with the *other* upon his return — that the boss's riddles and weird paperweights and the map of the city she is bent over are all coming together in her head and — but nope: the bab doesn't yet know what to do with the awful stories her map so meticulously records.

"The Market Hall, yo should see it!"

The bab's pretty sure that the Market Hall was shocked to its core by a bomb two months ago. The foremost informant this time is the 'Andy Carrier Lady, a shrivelled squint of a woman whose daytimes, before the bombs came, were spent on the steps of the Market Hall flogging 'andy carrier bags for a copper a pop. But with her, bending out behind her in a cabaret-style dance formation, are a number of accompanying stool pigeons: the Glory (or 'Glowery') woman, who for once is not warbling; a barrow boy without his barrow but with, by the gorgeous smell of it, a bag of hot baked potatoes; a man whom the bab has more than once seen paying for his apples by performing a series of gambols; and, at the rear, a sweaty policeman. The bab dutifully retraces the circle she made on her map the last time around. The Glory woman glowers at her. The 'Andy Carrier Lady starts to cry. The barrow boy wanders over to B3 and tries to flog him a baked potato. B3 is on the brink of giving in to the boy's sing-song persuasions and fishing a coin from his pocket when the policeman, whose role in the troupe has up until this point been ambivalent, intervenes. The policeman seems glad to have something to police. The gambol man, the bab notices, has vanished.

The reports keep coming.

"Blucher Street."

"Slade Road."

"Marshall & Snelgrove, well sort of. The doors of the public house opposite were sent soaring through our front windows. I thought the Corporation ought to know about it, that's all."

B3 coughs loudly.

"Hunter's Hill."

That's another one in B19. The bab tells herself she just better get used to this sort of thing.

"Armoury Road, Lozell's way."

The bab doesn't blink. Her pencil jumps a bit, but that's it. The oracle standing in front of her has a babba (not a bab) in one arm and a toddler eating the other. The bab (not the babba) does not dare look up at the oracle's fizzog, but notices that her nightie is dangling down below her overcoat. The overcoat is not at all raggedy. After the oracle and her brood have gone, the bab, in full view of the remaining and still considerable queue, nests her head in folded arms and gazes sideways at the set of framed photographs that Manzino had nailed onto the Enquiry Office wall. The pictures are of the city before the bab knew it, before the city was officially a city: before the incorporation the bab helped celebrate in the Grand. The pictures depict streets and squares and a squeezed 'gullet' — a choked passageway — that no longer exist.

The bab is not sleeping with Manzino, and never will be. It seems necessary to state that at this point.

The difference between the job the *other* did and the job the bab does is as follows. The bab has in front of her a map that is very big. It is not a map of the city as she thinks of it, which would be more or less messily-fried-egg-shaped but with a clear and defined centre, a healthily pulsing 'yoke.' Instead, the map Manzino has given her has multiple centres and multiple sprawls: it's a mess of many eggs fried in a pan simultaneously. It doesn't just show the city the bab would *say* she lives in. It shows the 'conurbation' — a bit of lingo she's recently picked out from the conversations of Manzino and B3 — that the city has turned into. It's essentially a diagram of many cities, or at least many towns, but the name of the city that the bab would *say* she lives in seems still to catch them all, to conglomerate and combine them. It's this conglomeration and combination that the bab has to cope with, but she does so, note, whilst remaining 'the bab.' She has not yet been, as the surveyors would say, 'coded', which in itself is code for 'promoted.' It is not clear how she could be. The job of Surveyor for Area Code B19 — i.e., the job of the *other* — was by contrast based solely in the smallish zone encompassed by B19, a mere blood clot in one of the bab's map's many egg whites. To do anything physical in B19, to construct in it, or to subtract structures from it to make room for new ones, you first had to speak to B19. Only through B19 (the *other*) could B19 (the area) be altered. Only by coming to the *other* with multiple planning applications could you build a new abattoir or pantry or whatever. So though the size of the *other*'s work zone was / is nothing compared to the area the bab's careful pencillings have to cover, the *other*'s work is / was arguably more 'constructive.' In short, the difference between the job the *other* did and the job the bab does is the difference between the two meanings of the word 'mortar.'

The bab is trying hard, but where B3 and Manzino see the skeletal structure of a new future, the bab sees only skeletons.

Though Manzino's road scheme is thought fantastically futuristic by those who know about it (not everybody does yet), the total area his inner ring road will encircle will be approximately equivalent to the total area spanned by the town way back in about 1780, before the town became a city.

The future annihilates the past. The past becomes the future.

"Biscuit?"

It's B3, offering the bab one of Manzino's leftovers. Groggy, snoozy, the bab looks confusedly up at him. The bab has no idea how long she has been asleep. The only indication is the wet patch on the sleeve of her cardigan. How on earth B3 has got hold of one of Manzino's rejects — fig rolls are an indulgence Manzino prefers not to advertise, because not everybody in Eden can expect a regular supply of biscuits — does not occur to her. It's probably not worth divulging.

B2

It's a short straight walk from the offices in Eden to the ODEON Cinema, where the bab often lunches in the restaurant above the cinema lobby, but each day now the walk is a different one. To the bab's mind, the bombs are like vicious children. Their violence is not arbitrary; they clobber the most important buildings first and then they go for the nicest, invariably the ones the bab has banked a tickle or transforming thought in, though those tickles and transforming thoughts are all much more present in her cranium now that the buildings that once contained them have been crushed, abolished, mortified. Luckily, the ODEON has so far stayed untouched. It has smooth faïence tiles (described by some as 'cream', others as 'buff', but agreed upon by all as a welcome disruption of the general grunge), a plushly furnished vestibule, and its name spelt out in lascivious red letters (no longer neon-lined at night, though). It really is very pleasant. Once the bab has stiletto-heeled her way across the roof tiles that these days cobble New Street, one half of a snapped snooker table, and, say, a toilet bowl tossed abroad from the Kardomah Café — once she has circumvented all the former *plus* the puckered lips and whistles of the teams of defusers and clean-uperers, then the ODEON offers solace. Its restaurant is lovely.

The waitresses who labour there refer to their place of work as 'the dolly-mixtures', paint their fizzogs with powder and loud lipstick, and wear pink blouses with pearly buttons. They are deep-throated and irrepressibly tender. All of them know the bab well, and are speedy in delivering her teapot, teaspoon, cup, saucer, roll and butter. The tea-strainer, its wire meshing well-scrubbed, all the little bits removed from the little holes in it, is never forgotten. About these sorts of things the bab is particular. If something goes missing, then instead of wiggling or being tugged by the lobe her ears get screwed into with a finger, which is not an appealing thing for a bab like the bab to be seen doing. The bab is a tad hesitant in issuing her order today, but then eats and drinks as normal. Her skirt kicks about under the table as she munches. To some this might convey nervousness, to others detached contentment.

"Top up?"

The bab's butter knife shivers like her pencil did earlier. Her unpinked lips pull off a movie-star tremble beautifully.

"Oh, no thank you. I'm waiting. For someone."

"Anyone special, bab?"

It is only the *other*, us, bus conductors and waitresses who call the bab 'bab.' It's not a term most of her colleagues would ever make use of, nor the bab of herself, for that matter. The bab isn't snobbish though, so this particular waitress is friendly to her.

"Just my father."

The bab keeps her eyes aligned firmly on the peak of her teacup. The waitress hovers, however. Her hair has a whisper of green in it — a sign that, at some point prior to her present position, she has been employed at the brassworks.

"He's doing well, thank you. I'm sure he'll be along soon!"

The waitress's scepticism, which from where the bab is sitting seems especially evident in the angle of her elbows, does little to reassure the bab.

"Can I get anything ready for him before he arrives, bab?"

The bab allows an eyebrow to lift, tilt, and relax again, all within a millisecond. The movement is studied but suffused with meaning, just as a raised eyebrow is in the movies.

"Just another cup will be fine."

As the waitress turns and walks, teapot bobbing, the bab clocks her bare legs and, eye-pencilled in down the back of them, a fat, brownish line. In the hollows behinds the knee-caps the line has smudged, become a skid-mark. It's because of sweat, presumably.

Time passes.

The bab spills tea on the tablecloth when she pours it and sees the tablecloth's pattern as streets plus Ordnance Survey gridlines. The brown spots of tea she takes for bombs.

Time passes.

From the pipes behind the bab's table comes the faint chanting of those who read out a movie's intertitles for those who don't know how to read them. The audience's voices grumble and swoon. The pipes collect the voices and incubate them, then after many years the voices leak back out again —

the voices the bab's ears are hearing must be old, she realises, because the movies are all talking now, not silent, as they were when the bab was a girl and her dad used to take her to matinees. There are no intertitles to read aloud, these days. It's the audience that's silent now.

The bab luxuriously sighs.

Time's passing is articulated by the ODEON clock in the corner, a clock that measures the intervals according to the ODEON letters instead of standard numerals. The bab was meant to meet her father here at big hand H little hand E, and it is presently big hand N little hand just past E.[1]

The bab wishes she had one of her pencils with her to scribble with.

The bab has had to smother a number of cinemas with her circles. The bombs rather fancy them: backed by enormous brick boxes, the spaces that contain the auditoriums, they are easily mistaken for fakterois from the skies. The cinemas further out in the suburbs spume up above the terraces like massive solidified fountains, and though the auditoriums are exquisitely formed on the inside — all green and orange carpets, stepped ceilings, glistening light fittings, combed plaster and rounded corners — the shape their mass makes is a dangerous one: their bulk resembles a warehouse. There's not much that can be done about it. One of the newer and huger suburban ODEONs employed an expert in camouflage

---

[1] 1=T; 12=H; 1=E; 2=/; 3=/; 4=N; 5=O; 6=E; 7=D; 8=O; 9=/; 10=/.

to make the cinema's rooftop look like the rooftops of houses. It was clever, but not bombproof. Twenty people were killed in the ODEON in B24. That bomb crunched down through the ceiling, crashing plaster all over the carpet and exploding on top of the sixpenny seats. The bab wishes she knew what movie had been showing, because perhaps if it was a boisterous one, one with cowboys, the bomb might have burst at exactly the moment when the hero was about to shoot his adversary. It would have been a wonderful effect, albeit macabre. The bab is both quite pleased with herself for thinking up this neat insertion of narrative meaning — or is the word 'continuity'? — into an otherwise savage 'cut', and at the same time disgusted. The ODEON she is in this moment has so far been fortunate. Its auditorium slots in amongst the shops and stores that line New Street: this ODEON is easily missable.

Time is becoming annoying.

The bab ponders the question of whether, if the person you are waiting for never arrives, then:

were you ever eigentlich *waiting for them?*

"Love."

It means 140 Armoury Road is alive.

"Dad!"

His eyebrows are alarmingly dusty and his stubble is at least two days old, but his collar and shoes are both brilliant. The bab gets up to give him a hug. He declines with a wobble and a faltering offering of his hand, which is, the bab now notices, as unwizened as B15's.

"How are you? There was a report in the Enquiry Office this morning..."

"..."

"?"

"..."

"How many digits have I got?"

The bab counts first her father's eyeballs and then the number of fingers and thumbs on his hands combined. It's ridiculous, but she can't help it. Her dad is an imaginary polydactyl: when she was little he used to get the bab to tell him how many digits he had on both hands together; when she said ten, he would nod solemnly, count down from ten the fingers and thumb on one hand − *10, 9, 8, 7, 6* − and then, scowling, hold up the other hand and declare 'plus 5 makes 11.'

"But you're fine? And mother and − Olsy?"

"Olsy is no longer with us."

"What?"

The bab has not been speaking to her older sister for some time. She's not sure which of them it was who originally sent the other to Coventry. There was no argument that she can recall, or at least not one with screeches and door-slams − but then those are not the kind of arguments the bab's family has ever had anyroad. Their arguments tend instead to take the form of silences that chug on for hours. As it happens their arguments often play out like a silent movie. The bab feels her insides jive. Her gullet impolitely raises the possibility of retroperistalsis.

"I mean to say she isn't living *with* your mother and I, not that she isn't living at all. Haw! How's that Manzino treating you?"

The bab sits herself down and again sighs, though not so luxuriously this time.

"Fine."

"Lots of work, I suppose."

"I suppose."

The bab's dad offers the bab a cigarette: she takes one, lets him light it, sucks at it once without inhaling, then stubs it out in the ODEON ashtray. The ashtray sizzles. The bab's eyes briefly settle on a poster for *Professor Mamlock* (dir. Adolf Minkin) pinned up on the wall opposite their table. Next to it, a little blistered, is a poster for *Hitler, Beast of Berlin* (dir. Sam Newfield). The bab's dad, the bab knows, will have seen both films already. He loves the movies. He goes most days, even now. The one thing the bab's dad has done that is sturdy enough to satisfy such a question as 'what does your dad *do*?' is to have helped found a film society along with a number of the pseudo-poets, -painters, and -sculptors he counts among his acquaintances. Though she has promised to, the bab has yet to go along to one of their salons in Livery Street.

Livery Street is long like a sad fizzog. It stretches down from Colmore Row almost all the way to B19, where

Armoury Road is. No bomb has so far fallen on it, but that doesn't matter; Manzino's new inner ring road is going to slice through it anyroad.

The bab misses the *other* very much.

The bab's father is named Doug. The bab never calls him that aloud and unlike the ODEON waitress he is not wearing a name-badge, but as it is good form to make a name known in this context— i.e. a fiction, a narrative, an account of something, my account of me— then 'Doug' shall the bab's dad be labelled. In the silent movies, by contrast, names were rarely necessary.

Since I am here I might as well say so. I *am*, after all, 'here.'

I, this city, this filthy city, this here filth, once saw a movie in which two people met and fell in love. It was made at about the time when the movies' primordial silence was itself being silenced, when sound technology was on the rise and all the silent stars were being forced to speak, to say something specific instead of crazily gesticulating. This movie, though, was a hybrid: most of it was soundless (apart from the score specially written for it and performed on the ODEON's neon organ). But then right in the middle of it, in a scene featuring some playful flirting on the beach, because this, unlike me, was a city by the sea and so a city with a beach — right in the middle of the movie, the movie started speaking. The world ripped, imperceptibly. The two of them continued flirting for a while, and then, almost as if they had no choice, almost as if their new-found sonic status had forced it upon them, almost as if the audible world could not cope with anonymity, they did this: they told each other their names. Two bodies on a beach became 'George' and 'Susan.' They, who by this point in the movie had been in love for at least two days, suddenly discovered it necessary to know each other's names. His voice was high-pitched, while hers was lewd and croaky. As soon as the soundwaves sank back out of their monochrome universe, they became again nameless, unindentified, without identity. I have sometimes wondered whether to their inhabitants silent movies are like nightmares: a grey mottled world where you scream but nothing comes out, where only a fraction of the things you say make it into the inter-titles. On the other hand, however, I have also wondered whether it is the talkies that are the true nightmare.

The bab groans. The way Doug is wagging his finger at one of the ODEON waitresses embarrasses her badly. The name-badged waitress who approaches their table is the same one who served the bab in the first place, but shall remain nameless. Leaning two hands on his stick, Doug watches the waitress's fingers elicit him his tea as a pet rodent oggles a proffered treat: with an interest that is genuine, yet utterly unpredictable in terms of commitment.

"Heard from him?"

He means the *other*, otherwise known as Surveyor for Area Code B19.

"No."

The bab blushes. Doug's raised chin refuses the roll the bab is offering him.

Doug is fond of the *other*. He is all for a marriage, though he doesn't care to announce so explicitly, with enthusiasm. To do so would be too crude. Doug doesn't do crude things. Though not deaf, Doug has trouble understanding what the *other* is saying. Their first exchange went stiltedly:

The *other*, nervous: "Awroight?"

Doug, baffled: "Oh, I'm very well, thank you so much for asking! Welcome to Armoury Road."

The *other*, equally baffled, plus now drunk on adrenalin and his first gulp of whiskey (he's a beer man usually and also an inveterate lightweight): "Sir, when the bab 'ere said I must come with her oop Armoury Road, yo know I thought she was spouting filth, like!"

Doug: "?"

Then Doug again, heartily amused: "Haw! Haw! Get the lad another whiskey!"

The *other*, to the bab: "Aw gosh, I'll be drunk as a boiled owl!"

Doug: "?"

The *other*, nudged by the bab in the ribs: "Soz, sir. I'd luv one."

'Awroight?' doesn't mean 'how are you.' It means 'hello.' It doesn't want or warrant any reply other than 'Awroight?'

In spite of these linguistic distances, the *other* and Doug tended — or tend: tense is after all a tender issue in these times — the *other* and Doug tend to get along wonderfully. In his capacity as Surveyor for Area Code B19, the *other* even assisted his dear bab's dad in making some alterations to the boarding house at 140: a new party wall to create two neat bedrooms where once there was one unnecessarily generous one; a basic but habitable attic conversion, etc. The *other* did some of the drafting work himself, a service in excess of his professional brief, and something that Manzino would not be pleased about if Manzino were to know about it. He would no doubt know it as 'moonlighting.' The Armoury Road boarding house itself is an establishment that Doug believes he runs, but which the bab's mom in reality resuscitates every morning at five *ante meridiem*, or big hand H little hand N, when Doug is just getting into bed. The bab's mom has never once commented on her husband's 'habits.' The bab would like to think that her mom's external sturdiness corresponds to an inner dominion equally robust, making her an oasis of mettle in a flood of familial friability, i.e. genealogical tendency to crumple, which in itself is a totally different thing to crumbling. It would be cruel and unnecessary to argue otherwise at this point.

The waitress fills Doug's teacup.

"Oscar Deutsch entertains our *nation!*"

"What?"

"I was admiring the lady's pouring. Oscar Deutsch is..."

"I know who Oscar Deutsch is."

Oscar Deutsch is the son of a local scrap metal merchant, a Hungarian Jew called Leopold.[2]

The bab tries to make it up to the departing waitress by smiling brightly at her skid-marks. The bab really wishes her father would not wag his finger at waitresses, but most of all she wishes he would do something, *something*, about the whiskey smell that drips from him. It doesn't do much more than drip — it doesn't hit her like a stampeding elephant or a sudden slap of November sunshine — but it does drip, and

---

[2]   And Oscar Deutsch, if you hadn't noticed, is also the man whose name lurks behind and in and between the ODEON cinema chain's logo, the man whose name the ODEON clocks cryptically tick to. It's a bit of a chicken and egg mystery as to which came first, Oscar Deutsch's ambitions to Entertain Our Nation or the ODEON chain and its slogan itself, but it's nonetheless the curious truth that Oscar went to school on the site of the very same cinema that the bab and Doug are currently sat in, and it is moreover the incontrovertible truth that, for all his untimely surname, Oscar Deutsch is a patriot of magnanimous proportions. At the bombs' outset, the foyers of all ODEON cinemas were set to work as recruiting stations for the Territorial Army. The bab's admiration for Oscar's creation — Oscar also being a distant acquaintance of the bab's dad — has been slightly ambivalated, if one can say so, by that fact. As in: she's not certain that sending men off to a de facto slaughter-house fulfils a promise to entertain a nation. The bab has much less sympathy these days for Oscar's famous yet unidentified ailment (a bit like Napoleon, Oscar D. is only ever seen in public with one hand hidden inside his shirt, clutching, presumably, his stomach). Btw., it's just occurred to me that ODEON half-rhymes with NAPOLEON, and that the latter is almost an anagram of LEOPOLD, the name of Oscar's father. LEOPOLD, NAPOLEON, NICKELODEON, ODEON. This is what too much time spent gazing into an ODEON clockfizzog does to you. Blooming 'eck, etc.

is noticed. The bab moreover feels that, somehow, the drip, drip, drip of her father's whiskey smell was a contributory cause of the silence that currently exists between her and her sister, Olsy. If anywhere in their boarding house in any of the multiple rooms a tap was dribbling, or even hinting that it might dribble in the near future, Olsy could never sleep. The bab and Olsy shared a room together until Olsy was nearly nineteen. At fifteen, Olsy started wearing lipstick louder than an ODEON waitress's and inviting boarders into the bedroom for cups of imaginary tea. At fifteen and a half she switched the imaginary tea for whiskey and started letting the boarders kiss her. Whenever this began to happen the bab would begin to leave the bedroom, but as soon as Olsy saw her tiptoeing, she would put a stop to the kissing and demand that the bab sit back down.

Olsy was fabulous, the boarders were always telling the bab.

"Have you heard from Frank?"

Frank is the bab's younger brother. He went to school with Oscar Deutsch's only son. He wants to be an architect but can't yet, because of the bombs.

"Nothing from Frank."

The bab nods simply. According to the ODEON clock it's O to /, but what the bab sees now is what it says on her own watch, which neatly announces that it's twenty to two. Though the watch's strap is surprisingly shabby for someone so carefully turned out, the watchfizzog itself is as immaculate as it was the day the *other* bought it for the bab from one of the watch shops over in Icknield Street.

The shop in question was one among many, all of them equally glittery with clocks and watches. The shops hadn't looked much like shops, though: they had looked like small, scrambling houses out of which the chores and rhythms of domesticity had only gradually been eliminated, so that what had once been homes with workshops out in the backyard had at last transformed themselves into workshops and trading rooms completely. The twinkling bay windows gestured at being shop-fronts, but only vaguely. When the bab and the *other* stepped through the first door that took their fancy, the bab got the feeling that she was intruding into the house not of someone desperate to remember something, as you might expect from all the time-keeping machinery everywhere, but instead to *forget* something. To utterly forget it. Hooked, perched, nailed, pinned, caged in glass and packaged in boxes, the clocks and watches confused time, bewildered it, sent it all over the shop. In their multitude, these instruments no longer kept time. With no intervals between them, a tick or a tock no longer kept anything. In that shop, amid the incessant ticking of so many clocks, time was all but lost.

"Isn't it strange, the way we speak."

"?"

"I mean — why do we say that we *keep* time? With a watch. Or when we're dancing. What is there about time to *keep*?"

The bab hadn't much enjoyed it, this feeling that had crept up on her, but when she tried to explain the feeling to the *other*, the *other* only hiccupped and declared her to be squeamish. In the teashop they went to afterwards, the bab wasn't able to explain how she couldn't see how the *other* could apply the quality of squeamishness to a discomfort essentially concerned with the ability of objects to imply the opposite of their immediate function (or something).

There were plenty of ordinary jewellers on Icknield Street, but the *other* had made a fuss about not buying the bab a ring to mark their engagement. He'd said a ring would be a) too ominous; b) too conspicuous; and c) too reminiscent of his rival, which meant Manzino. For all her wonder at the *other*'s assumption that she actually cared whether she wore a ring, watch, or Hoola Hoop, the bab had considered a) a sensible enough reason given the *other*'s impending and potentially deathly departure; b) semi-sensible, because though they did not want everybody to know yet, the bab would happily have worn the ring on the wrong hand if necessary; but then c) ridiculous. Ever since the centenary celebrations, when the bab had danced once and badly with Manzino in the Grand's marblecake ballroom, the *other* had made Manzino his sworn enemy and competitor in perpetuity. He apparently imagined the bab to be entertaining fantasies of a life of easy grandeur spent fizzing around the city in a specially fitted-out Austin motorcar, and on Friday evenings hosting dinner parties for all the cronies from the local outpost of the RIBA — even though Manzino, as an engineer, is not a member of the Royal Institute of British Architects anyroad. The bab took quiet offence that the *other* could think such things of her. That said, she has recently had some trouble negotiating her thoughts regarding Manzino's fireplace. What's that all about?

The *other* didn't drive a motorcar. He rode a bicycle and was saving up to buy a motorcycle. The fakteroi that made the other's bicycle also manufactured small arms. Now it was making gunlocks and shellfuses, gearboxes and tank engines, stuff that the *other* and Frank had been sent off to put a stop to the bombs with.

The *other* had not wanted to go.

To summarise:

The bab and the *other* are engaged to be married.

The bab wears an engagement watch instead of an engagement ring. When all the clockfizzogs around tell the time by the ODEON letters, this is useful.

The bab's dad, Doug, is unaware of the engagement (we don't know for sure about her mom).

The bab assumes her dad would disapprove of the *other* as marriage material, despite the two of them getting along famously.

The bab is consequently afraid to tell her dad of the engagement. (But is that what she's really afraid of?)

The bab's dad secretly hopes that the bab and the *other* will get married, but won't ever say so voluntarily.

Olsy, a woman of no fixed location (possibly off the bab's map completely), is pregnant by an unknown soldier. Of this both the bab and her dad, Doug, are for the moment unconscious.

Their teacups plumbed to the depths and their rolls and butter decimated, the bab and Doug automatically rise from the table. A pink vase filled with flowers starts to tumble, but then, at the very last moment, doesn't. The flowers' stems must have metal wires in them (the bab reckons that's the only way the flowers could stay so upright). Considering this, the bab does back up the top button of her cardie. This top button is different to the others. It's a pretty bit of nothing given her by her mom who got it from her mom.The bab has always admired the button's checkerboard pattern. It doesn't match either her outfit or the ODEON carpet, but the fact that it rarely matches anything is why the bab likes it. The *other* once told her the button's pattern bore a resemblance to the grid of a city; which city, the bab can't remember. It definitely wasn't this one.

The bab makes a mess of the buttoning for thinking. Doug watches her absently. Heavily greased, his hair needs combing.

The nameless name-badged waitress nips briskly across the room, the bab and Doug's bill of fare wafting in the breeze brought on by her movements.

"Doug?"

Doug's chin has slumped to his neck, a gesture made to facilitate bill-inspection. He perks up when the bab addresses him.

"Yes?"

"I hope you hear from Frank soon."

"Yes."

Doug's chin sinks again.

"Dad?"

Lifts again.

"Yes?"

"I'll write to Olsy. I'm sure I can find out her address."

Sinks again.

"Yes. After all, you're the one with the map."

Doug's attempts at making light of the bab's career trajectory feel almost as cruel as B3's, if at the same time more forgivable. The bab even manages to shove a snort through her nostrils. Doug does not stop staring at the tear of paper that represents their bill. The bab knows he is attempting to 'stare it out', literally. It's a sight she finds both saddening and distasteful, mainly saddening. Olsy would just find it dull.

"Dad, I'll pay."

The offer, though, is futile. The bab leaves Doug wandering towards the till, his shoulders impeccably arranged, his stick swishing at long-ago perfected angles. He will spend ten to fifteen minutes enquiring about the till-boy's family and favourite colour, congratulate him on his smart collar, stun him with reminiscences of movies the boy has read about in the old movie magazines he finds rotting in the ODEON's projection room, and then leave the restaurant without paying. That is Doug's way.

REDEVELOPMENT

B14

There is pain and there is blood. There is hurting — crass, zipping, *hot* — and there is blood. There has been an explosion of blood. All over his shirt and all over his bum — because he mechanically did what he does when his hands get dirty: he wiped them on his shirt and his bum — there is blood. There is blood everywhere except where blood should be: pooling on his skin instead of swimming inside it, spreading through the cotton threads of his sleeve instead of through his capillaries, splashing out from his wrist when he shakes it wildly — as if to shake off what has been lost, as if to get it off him, this terrible loss, his wrist is wildly shaking. There is pain — crass, zipping, *hot* — and there is blood.

The young man known as Zero has cut off his hand.

Zero (real name: Terence) has cut off his hand. In the wire fakteroi where he works — but that's not what Zero sees right now, cos Zero isn't seeing clearly at all.

In a silvery space in B14, Zero stands, shocked. In a space where time has paused and then crazily winked at him — everywhere he looks, there are glittery orbs, winking — Zero has experienced something properly awful, something he's often thought about, but never been able to take in as a real possibility. Zero's done one of those things that only ever happens to other people. He's cut off his hand. Amidst the ping and glint of silvery machinery, he stands, shocked.

Zero (he originally wanted to call himself 'Zero.' as in 'Zero Point' but the 'Point' bit wasn't as catchy as plain 'Zero', it turned out) — Zero is the kind of boy-becoming-young-man who thinks, or up until recently thought, that pain is something it's necessary to get a handle on. That pain is something to be managed, applied, and controlled was, up until a few moments ago, one of Zero's most treasured wisdoms. And believe him, he's had plenty of it — pain — to know so.

The pain, for example, of having a real name like 'Terence' and yet wanting to be as rock and roll as possible.

The trick, thought Zero, was not to *feel* pain, but to work it. Put the pain to work. Just as the only way to get through a day in the fakteroi without voluntarily hacking your hands off was not to think of yourself as working *for someone* but instead as *working something*, whether it be dead metal or whatever, the game with pain, Zero reckoned, was to work it. In Zero's own experience, the most terrible thing about pain is that it's alien. Despite it coming at you so fast and hard, your pain is never yours. Like the fierce hatred you suddenly feel towards a friend for no good reason other than the way he's tapping his fag ash into the ashtray, pain comes at you from nowhere, a foreign body, a slut-farthing. This is terrible and terrifying. And so the best way to deal with pain, Zero up until recently reckoned, is therefore to get a handle on it.

In Zero's case, this has in the past meant doing things

like snatching the fag off the friend who's tapping it and extinguishing said fag on his (Zero's) forearm. Or, stepping up to your room after another speechless meal shared with your gran (Zero lives with his gran in a two-up-one-down back-to-back, Lozells way) — stepping up the wooden staircase to your room and by candlelight, by candlelight in all senses, adding another angry circle to the proud flesh already scarring your forearm. For Zero, self-applied pain has become been a way out, a transformation. A lever. A way of taking control. Instead of wincing when his gran got rid of one of his rotten molars by tying it to the door by a string and telling him to stand dead still and then slamming the door so that the tooth tore out of his gob and flew after the door trailing blood behind it — instead of wincing Zero simply relaxed into the experience. Levered it. Closed his eyes and imagined it was he himself who was slamming the door shut. One of Zero's favourite mottos was (until a few seconds ago) this: if it's chilly in your thin bed at night, don't shiver, cos shivering will only make you colder. Zero is a young man for whom control is very important. But levers need hands to guide them. And, as it happens, Zero is an ace guitarist. The loss of his left mawler is the one thing he can't handle.

Apart from the arm he is waving (he can't control the waving: he can't make it stop), Zero is standing completely still. Around him weave glittery orbs. This is because the metal machines — the reels with the coiled pickled billets; these reels releasing wire to the cylindrical drums on the spindles; the vises; on the vises the die the wires pass through (the dies being what shrink the wire's diameter); the machines that mark the grooves in and then where Zero is standing the cutters, the cutters that cut the wire rods to size — the metal machines are no longer solid structures, but constellations of dots. The machines have became dots. Zero's workmates have become dots. The old man who works next to Zero, for instance: instead of a crooked old man in a red-tinted vizor, Zero sees now a sprinkle of dots. The shapes, elbows, stretches, angles, creases, rolls, rods, even the wires, even the grooves in the wires, even the wires that have been cut and gathered and stacked in the corner ready to be stored: all these objects have become dots. Zero can see nothing but dots.

Space has atomized.

Time has paused.

For the young man manically waving his wrist at nobody, time no longer counts. As Zero swings his arm back and forth something within him has already realised that:

There'll be no more clocking in and clocking out. There'll be no more perforations in a square card, no more punched circles in the blue card Zero slots, each morning, into the slitty mouth in the box on the wall. There'll be no pedal cycles from his gran's two-up-one-down and no more perforations in his card because time, now, doesn't count. Zero has cut off his hand and might as well for all he knows be standing submerged in a can of beer or tin of pop: all around him metal is bending. Against a curving background of silvery metal spin winking orbs. There is fizz. There is bend and curve. There is — fizzy pop.

This is what has happened to Zero (this is what it feels like to him right now): Zero has cut off his hand and then been plunged through a circular opening (sharp around the rim) into a tin of pop (the can of beer recedes, and now Zero thinks only of things he thought of when he was seven years old). There has been an explosion of tomato sauce: Zero smacked the aristotle right on the mark just as he did the first time his gran bought tomato sauce and they ate it dolloped over *airship in clouds* (sausage and mash).

Zero was brought up by his grandmom in her two-up-one-down back-to-back because Zero's mom was killed by a bomb when Zero was barely one week old. Zero's gran has one glass eye. It twinkles if you gobble your food.

Zero, who remembers nothing about any bombs, but who grew up playing in the holes the bombs bored, used to have a repeating nightmare about his gran's glass eye. In the nightmare the glass eye exploded when his grandmom was standing in her paved yard, which in the dream became a back garden, turfed and flowerbedded, and when the grandmom's eye exploded all the glass fragments sprayed out and stuck in the mud beneath the pansies. Why pansies, who knows. In his dream Zero pulled the fragments out of the ground one by one, even though as he did so the shards transformed into fat blue worms like the ones he'd seen above his grandma's knees when he'd accidentally walked in on her undressing, yuk.

He'd heard somewhere — probably at school, where the boys in his class started smoking fags when they were seven years old — Zero had heard somewhere that all babies began as a twinkle in their dad's eye. For Zero, whose mom was killed by a bomb when he was one week old and who never knew his dad at all, this was an explanation of his point of origin profoundly difficult to understand. It made the pins that stabbed from his grandmom's glass eye all the more painful.

Breathe, Zero.

All over his shirt and all over his bum — because he mechanically did what he does when his hands get dirty: he wiped them on his shirt and his bum — is blood.

There are also dots. There are glittery orbs.

There is not a sound.

There has been an explosion of blood.

As Zero waves his arm across this tinselly spacescape, it suddenly comes to him that if he has cut off his hand then there will be no more *guitar*.

And then the clockfizzog on the wall dares to tick one tiny tick, and when it does, Zero screams.

His scream is thin and sharp. It's so thin and so sharp that it slices the room, tearing down all the tinsel, so that now instead of silvery space there is only the dull horrid bloat of a space which because of that clock tick has again begun to churn (with time). And because he doesn't want it to start again yet — the world can't start again until he gets this terrible loss off him — Zero screams. His scream is so sharp it almost cuts off the ears of his workmates, who now turn away from their positions over the machinery and, with eyes slowly widening, watch Zero. To them this young man Zero, who's so quiet usually, who's such an easy, amicable presence to have around the fakteroi, who's all right 'really', some of the workers sometimes add, with a nasty look in their eyes — to them Zero is now standing very still apart from one strangely thrashing arm, screaming.

Zero screams.

His workmates gawp.

And then the clock dares to tick one, two, three ticks, and then, when it's about to tick some more, Zero starts to yell. His yell is as heavy and thick as a concrete wall.

"Get it off!"

"Ooooowwww! Ooooom!"

"Get it *off* of me!"

"*Shite.* Somebody get it *off*!"

Across the other side of the fakteroi floor, a man who's worked in the fackeroi for yonks spikes a bony elbow into the side of the man standing next to him, whispers:

"What's the kid on about?"

But the man standing next to the man can do nothing but gawp.

"What's he on about?"

"What's wrong with his arm?"

All across the floor, elbows spike into ribcages. The

space that was once tinselly with winks and dots, now is tinselly with whispers.

"Oi."

"I know."

"What — ?"

"Gawd."

"I — dunno."

It's this: Zero is thrashing his arm and yelling what he's yelling because via some strange spasm of nerves he's become convinced that what the end of his arm *has lost* is something he has got to *get off him*. That is, he is trying wildly to shake the loss off. As if a snake had swallowed his hand and stuck in its fangs and not let go, Zero is desperately trying to shake what has happened to him *off* of him (when he was seven years old Zero saw some snakes in a glass cage in the zoo: he saw their fangs and imagined what it would be like to have his hand bitten by one). And though what he is yelling sounds pretty odd to his workmates, who can see only a bloody arm thrashing about, what he is yelling is, if you think about it, only the vocal expression of what most people automatically do when pain has bitten them. When you miss the metal nail and bang your thumb, what do you do? Exactly: you shake your hand. When you slam a door (or a door slams) and you catch the tips of your fingers in the closing gap, what do you do? You shake your hand: what you do is you try to shake the pain off. The only difference between that and what Zero's doing now is that it's not the pain that Zero is trying to shake off. Standing there submerged again in dots and winks and twinkles, *Zero is trying to shake off what he has lost.*

Now a man is by his side. Now the man is gone. It's the man in the red-tinted vizor coming to and fro towards and away from Zero as if he's on the end of a yo-yo Zero's throwing: suddenly distant, suddenly close, suddenly distant, suddenly close. As he comes close, the man grabs Zero by the shoulder of his good arm and speaks into his ear:

"Calm down now."

The man springs away.

The man bounces back. Another man comes. The two men hold Zero by one shoulder each. Another man comes. This one squeezes Zero's elbow, the grinding elbow of the thrashing arm. Zero struggles, groans.

"Get it — *off.*"

'Calm down now."

"That's it."

"Hold *still.*"

Zero shudders. Hoarsely, he groans. At last, he allows himself to be led away from his position by the cutting machine and seated. The men seat him on a small wooden chair near to where the wires are stacked. The men don't call the wires 'wires', though, they call them *bars*: instead of the kind of wires that bend into an umbrella, or piano wires, or wires for toys of various sorts, the fakteroi where Zero works produces wire of far thicker gauge. It's the kind of wire that snakes through concrete and that keeps the concrete where it should be: rebars, reinforcement. The fakteroi signed a manufacturing contract with the Corporation a year or so ago. The bars stacked by where Zero is sitting are for reinforcing the new road. The contract called the road the A4400, but everybody Zero knows knows it as the inner ring road.

"Put him here, by the bars."

Carefully arranged in layers, cross-hatched, the bars have tiny grooves in them: that's how they grip the concrete. It was one of these that Zero was cutting when his mind suddenly slipped (but Zero's mind *never* slips when he's working — Zero tries now to recall what it was his mind slipped on) and when his mind slipped so did his fingers and now the clock has started to tick again: all across the fakteroi floor, elbows are going back to work. The elbows bend against machinery that gurgles, whirls: metal is pulled, passed through, drawn, pulled, passed on and eventually cut. The wires are drawn and the wires are cut.

Zero's head nods.

What was it his mind slipped on?

Dots.

A palm slaps him.

Zero involuntarily burps, opens his eyes, buries them in a frown. All of a sudden he feels irritable.

"Ow. That hurt."

Dots.

His mind slipped on — what?

The glass eye of Zero's gran is now orbiting Zero very

slowly, never blinking. There it goes again now: never, ever, blinking.

Another slap.

"Oi, get yer mawlers off of me!"

The crooked old man in the red vizor laughs. His teeth are yellowy brown. The two front ones are snapped in half.

"Best stay awake now. No good kipping now: yower losing a fair bit of blood."

"I...what?"

The man in the red vizor bends, squats, bounces on his heels, points. At the end of Zero's arm there's a tremendous swelling: instead of a hand, a turbaned shirt, already oozy with blood, has been attached to the wrist Zero was previously waving. Zero blinks, peers at the man, considers punching him in the chest with the bloody glove. The man's chest is bare.

"Have I...?"

The bars Zero is sitting by are thick steel wires. They are for pouring concrete into: they are for reinforcing concrete. They form what is called the concrete's carcass and —

"Why am I sitting down?"

"Lad..."

— and sometimes that is how the men Zero works with speak of the wire that's been cut and stacked: they either speak of the 'bars', or they speak of the stacked bars collectively as 'the carcass', even though there's no concrete poured in amongst the bars yet.

Zero is sweaty. The circle of proud flesh on his arm, the

scary whorl formed by fag burn and candle fire — this circle seems now to be pulsing.

"*Carcass.*"

Zero says it. He's said it so many times and yet it's never seemed so strange to him. Why do they call it a *carcass*?

"*Carcass?*"

"Not to worry now lad, they've gone to get Tis 'im. It won't be long till yower out of here, like."

"No, I."

"What's that?"

"*Carcass.*"

Zero whispers the word, incants it. His mind slipped and so did his fingers. What was it his mind slipped on?

The eyes behind the red vizor lean in on him.

"What's that? A car crash? No lad, not a car crash. Just a small accident, like."

"Small?"

And now that he pauses to think about it, Zero realises that the turbaned shirt at the end of his wrist is *wrapped around something*. He can't have cut off his hand.

"Ar, yow've sliced through two of yower fingers, like."

There is pain.

There are dots.

Now, who would have thought that momentous realisations can be born of portable staplers?

The ww was searching for the portable stapler because she wanted to staple together a supplement that had come with *The Post* that day. *Supplement* was the word for a newspaper spread that was independent and relatively expansive, i.e. an extended feature that took up too much room to be included in the paper normally. A supplement was basically a sort of growth or nodule: secondary (it owed its existence to the paper it came with) yet separate (it existed on its own in its own right, a closed system). It was not a discursive newspiece. Its close cousin was the 'insert.' In contrast to the rest of the paper, a supplement often contained many sizeable pictures, sometimes in colour. For *The Post* they were a fairly new phenomenon and the ww, since two years now, was in the habit of collecting them. The fifty or so supplements she had so far gathered were stacked in a pile in her boxy bedroom next to the airing cupboard. The ww's bedroom really was box-shaped: shoe-box shaped. Twigs tinkled her window at night. There was a space for a sink, but no sink. A nail the ww had once inserted into the wall remained permanently relieved of any burden. Because it was next to the airing cupboard, the ww's room often overheated. It got hot and stuffy in there.

Compared to the way the rest of the ww's things

were distributed across her bed, desk, and floorspace, the supplement pile was always kept very neatly. The ww's mom, who was still straightforwardly the ww's mom at the point at which the ww was searching for the portable stapler, had been instructed never to move it, the pile, even when cleaning. If she had to clean, she should 'mow' around the pile at a safe distance. 'To mow' was the verb the ww's mom had once used instead of 'to Hoover' (she owned a small vacuum cleaner, a 'De Luxe 652'). The ww's mom had a bit of a thing about switching words around, was always doing it: some of the words her tongue blundered into were so amusing/apposite/ somehow more precise or evocative than the right word would have been that they stuck and soon came into common familial usage.

Anyroad. The ww never *eigentlich* read any of the supplements she collected, so in terms of their subject matter she was indiscriminate. Whether one contained football analysis or an exploration of contemporary fashion trends (neither topic holding much appeal for her), the ww slid the supplement out and kept it. It was true that she sometimes leafed through the pages, especially if the pictures were in colour. Usually, though, she simply extracted a supplement from the newspaper it came in and, after stapling it carefully with the portable stapler, placed it on the top of the pile in her bedroom. The supplements that came with *The Post* were still at this point relatively lightweight[1] and mostly came unstapled. They couldn't have been called *magazines*, yet. A magazine typically had more than one subject; the supplements the ww collected had one theme or organising principle maximum. They were more concentrated than magazines, more obsessional. The pile in the ww's bedroom was organised according to date of publication only. That was the one rule she had. As soon as one supplement had been superseded in the pile by another, the ww never touched it again. She never retrieved any of the buried supplements, let alone sat down on one of the floral settees in her parents' living-room and *eigentlich* re-read one.

That said, there was one supplement, once, whose subject really caught the ww's attention. It was dedicated to a discussion of 'pyschoanalysis', which, prior to the marginal notices on *The Post*'s front cover alerting readers to the forthcoming supplement (ads that ran for a week or so), was not a word the ww had ever heard or come across before. It wasn't even a German word: the ww knew this because she had gone to the trouble of looking it up in her German dictionary.

This particular supplement was slightly weightier than average and sought to explain the basic principles of psychoanalysis (which turned out to be mind medicine, according to the supplement's first paragraphs) to a 'generally general audience.' 'Generally general' was the way the author

---

[1] In terms of weight. Of the supplements' profundity I'm saying nothing.

described his or her audience. This phrase alone had made the ww's mind go gambolling. Anyroad. The supplement also embarked on a discussion of how psychoanalysis worked in practice. It described what an appointment was ('appointment' wasn't the word the author used: it was something more like 'session'); where you were positioned when you were in one of these sessions (there was a room with a day bed or 'couch' in it and you lay on the couch though in theory it was supposed to be up to you where you put yourself, 'you' being the 'analysand' and the one other person present in the room being the 'analyst'); what you chatted about (your childhood; your dreams; your foibles).There were some pictures too: one monochrome reproduction of a photo of an empty room; one of a similar room but now with two people sitting/lying in it (the caption read 'psychoanalysis in action': the ww wasn't totally certain whether this was supposed to be humorous); and one abstract drawing, a constellation of squiggles of which the ww could make neither head nor tail. This drawing the ww had showed to her mom. Her mom had put down her rope-net shopping bag (she had only just got back from the butcher's), scrunched her eyes (she was without her reading glasses), and observed that what it reminded her most of was the shorthand forms she had used when she worked as a secretary. In reply, the ww surmised that the abstract drawing was intended to be suggestive of the pyschoanalytic experience, i.e. it was intended to be suggestive of what your mind might feel like if you yourself were an analysand reclined on a daybed recounting your dreams plus foibles. This interpretation the ww had come up with as the smell of raw faggots had wafted up to her nostrils from the shopping bag that lay slumped on the doormat.

Do not suppose the ww wasn't aware that her pile of supplements had something melancholic about it.

But even the supplement about psychoanalysis was eventually deposited atop the pile and then in its turn supplanted. After two years of collecting, the pile was becoming increasingly precarious. In the ww's boxy bedroom next to the airing cupboard, the pile was positioned in the relative expanse between the ww's bed and her wardrobe. This was why the ww's mom could, as well as had to, circle round it whenever she was mowing. To begin with the system had worked fine, but at over fifty supplements the pile's neatness was rapidly diminishing. The top part began to veer leftwards. The covers of supplements once buried began to show themselves. As with a deck of cards slowly splayed, or a horizontal gravestone slid sideways, what once was concealed now revealed itself. To walk within the pile's force field (you just sort of had a feel for what constituted this) was to threaten its stability with turbulence. In magnitude the pile was now elephantine. A new pile therefore appeared on the ww's brown carpet not long after the psychoanalysis supplement had been deposited.

The psychoanalysis supplement was perhaps third or maybe fourth from the top of the old pile when the new pile was started. For a while there existed two extremely lopsided stacks in the ww's bedroom: while one reached a mole situated midway between the ww's kneecap and hipbone, the other was about level with the highest point of her little toe. And yet even when this new pile consisted of one solitary supplement (about motorcars), the ww's mom was wise enough to mow around it instead of moving it, this solitary supplement, which of course she could have done easily. The ww's mom was patient in that way. 'Patient', as the ww herself realised, wasn't really the right word, though, because rather than tolerating her child's foibles, it was more as if the ww's mom unquestioningly accepted their seriousness. The glossy supplement with the car beaming out from its cover (the motorcar was an Austin), this really was an island that the mower must not mow across. The ww's mom truly believed in the ww's arrangement of reality. She took the pile as seriously as a roadblock. And in so doing, the ww's mom was herself childlike.

Anyroad. Do not think it escaped the ww's notice that this interest of hers in newspaper supplements was a bit on the strange side. It was strange in part because what most obviously characterised the interest was, *eigentlich*, a lack of interest. Apart from the one about psychoanalysis, and apart from the pleasure she felt when thumbing through the pictures, the ww wasn't in the slightest concerned with the content of the supplements. The point was their accumulation. That was all. And yet this lack of interest in the supplement's contents, each one's internal, as it were, *purpose*, was odd. Usually the ww read loads. She was one of those young adults who are said to 'devour' books. Her school reports went so far as to describe her as 'voracious.' After two years of collecting, there was still no question of the ww stopping, but at the same time the two lopsided stacks in her boxy bedroom next to the airing cupboard were becoming a quiet embarrassment, something that sometimes troubled the ww's consciousness when she was out somewhere, at a dance for instance, or taking an exam, etc. For some reason the piles never bothered her when she was alone with them in her bedroom. When they were right there, she hardly noticed them. It was more that they would arise whenever she was trying to be a person other than the person who had spent two years hoarding supplements without even reading them.

The whole thing became faintly painful, or as the Germans put it, *peinlich*.

And yet the ww kept on collecting. Her mom continued to mow around the piles, never moving them but never mentioning them either. In this way she acted more as a mom does towards the bedsheets of a son who has recently started masturbating. I.e., the ww's mom started acting less like a child and more like an adult who understands that people have passions and feelings that are neither necessarily present to other people nor necessarily comprehensible to the person whose passions and feelings they are in the first place. In this way the ww's mom proved herself to have an excellently developed *theory of mind*; moms usually do. They see there's something there that they themselves can't see, and, most movingly, they adapt themselves to this gap in their world with grace and sensitivity. They (moms) recognise another person's mental territory in the same way people who have never been to a certain country nevertheless recognise that country's existence. Fathers, by contrast, tend not to be too good at putting themselves in another person's shoes, and instead tend to go about squeezing other people into their own shoes.

That's not always the case, of course.

And that's not to say the ww didn't masturbate.

All this was all before the ww discovered her birth certificate. And yet the ww came across her birth certificate because she was searching for the portable stapler, with which she intended to staple the supplement that had come with *The Post* that day.

The ww in general never read the supplements, but being otherwise a voracious reader and also a bit of a thinker, she did try to get past the aspect of embarrassment and sort out what was happening to the best of her ability. In other words, she attempted to put her feet up on an imaginary couch and discuss her foibles.

First of all, it hadn't escaped the ww's notice that the collecting of the supplements had started around the same time of her dad's retirement.

For most of her childhood, the ww's dad had eaten a perfunctory breffus of buttery toast buttered on both sides accompanied by two poached eggs, drunk three mugs of tea, and cycled off to Eden, where he worked as some sort of surveyor or something for the Corporation. He returned home every lunchtime for the main meal of the day, and then went back off to the office. In the evenings, after an early supper and glass of beer, which the ww's dad preferred to whiskey, the dining table was transformed into a drawing board. There, assisted by the ww until she became too old and started to find it ridiculous, the ww's dad compiled plans for an imaginary city. The plans were immaculately detailed. As well as the masterplan, which was revised over and over, its shape repeatedly reformed in sketchbooks and on elephant-sized paper, there also existed endlessly perfected plans for this imaginary city's various zones, even for individual buildings, each of which always had a clearly assigned function. The ww's job was to sharpen her dad's carefully kept pencils and, sometimes, to colour in segments of these plans according to his specific directions. What the ww found most remarkable about this project (which the ww for a long time considered far more interesting than whatever it was her dad did when he went off to Eden) was that, as revision followed revision, the imaginary city her dad was planning came to look less like a city than the absence of one. The ww couldn't say why this was, exactly. The plans were incredibly detailed, as already mentioned. In early versions, the masterplan appeared to have been based on the physiognomy of an octopus, the ww's dad's favourite sea-born animal, but over time the tendrils had tapered off while the central eyeball had become a teardrop, detached from its bodily socket. Thereupon the plan started more to resemble a jellyfish. Apart from the barest suggestion of there being something sketchily present, this imaginary city her dad was planning had gradually become practically invisible. This made the ww feel queasy.

It also gave the ww the creepy yet familiar feeling that her dad was *eigentlich* more interested in getting rid of the things he was thinking about than he was in bringing them into existence.

Anyroad.

The only other thing that was in any way remarkable about the ww's dad was that he rode a bicycle even though he only had one real, flesh and blood leg. Each morning after his poached eggs the ww's dad cycled off to Eden with a contraption, specially constructed by the ww's dad himself, strapped to the wooden stump that was in turn strapped to what remained of his thigh flesh. The contraption looked a little akin to a mousetrap. The ww's dad called it his 'frigmajig.' He could be observed attaching it in the hallway with the same swift elegance of gesture with which he had only two seconds ago put his hat on, although the smoothness of his movements ceased as soon as he'd tipped his hat (he tipped it to nobody: he simply tipped it) and started clacking his way towards the front door.

The ww had never ever heard her dad express discontentment regarding his leg situation. That said, she had never heard him express much of anything whatsoever.

But then, two years ago, there had been an accident. It wasn't a car crash or any sort of road accident, but something to do with the new tower blocks whose construction the ww's dad was overseeing as part of his job with the Corporation. After a nervous period spent in hospital, when it looked like he might have to sacrifice a second leg, which would have left him totally legless but not in a fun way, the ww's dad was given early retirement. For two years now, the ww's dad had been pogo-sticking it around the rooms and stairwells of the semi-detached cottage[2] they lived in, his prosthetic metal-capped

---

[2] It wasn't really a cottage, obviously. The ww and her parents co-habited in a complex of houses and sweetshops and two adjoined tennis courts built some yonks before the bombs. It was a miniature version of the sort of development widely referred to as a 'Garden Suburb.' The houses had roofs that looked thatched but which weren't thatched. That sort of thing. Testament to the houses' timezone of construction were the small white nubbins discoverable in every room except the pantry and scullery. Easily mistaken for electric light switches, these small white nubbins were *eigentlich* bells by which to summon the (non-existent) servants: mounted above the scullery doorway was the hub of the system, a sort of switchboard, which informed you in which room what bell was ringing. That their house had once been the kind of house that people with servants lived in had, understandably, fascinated the ww. She had spent many gleeful afternoons 'chasing the bells down', as she called it, a game that involved punching the nubbin in, say, the bathroom, where there was a bell designed to be reach-able for someone taking a dunk in the bathtub, and then trying to sprint downstairs and into the scullery in time to see the corresponding bell above the doorway ringing. (In reality the bell corresponding to the bathroom manically vibrated but made no sound whatsoever. The circuit was faulty.) It was, of course, an impossible endeavour that the ww had set herself. But

and his good foot tartan-slippered. The combination of shag, tile, stone, cork dust and linseed oil on sisal backing (lino), plus the constant alternation of slipper-step and metal-step, meant that the sound of the ww's dad moving through these spaces was unusually cacophonous. His presence turned the house into a percussion instrument, an effect his practice of tapping at the walls to check their 'soundness' only augmented. For her last two years of school, which were also her first two years of collecting supplements, the ww's newly retired dad simply did not know what to do with himself. He stopped working on his imaginary city in the evenings. He even went so far as to remove his prosthetic and use it, inverted, to tap at the ceilings, though admittedly he mostly did this when the ww and Zero were together in her boxy room next to the airing cupboard. It was only when the well in the yard caved in — but that was not until later, literally the day before the ww unearthed her birth certificate — that her dad found something to do. Up until the well incident, the ww's dad was like a clock that's continuously ticking but no longer tells the time, and whose tick therefore becomes an irritant, even a torment. This was the exact way the ww described her dad in her diary: as a clock that's continuously ticking but no longer tells the right time. It wasn't a very nice analogy and she felt bad that she'd thought of it. He was repetitive and inflexible, yes, but generally

---

then, impossibility is what children's games are built to teach us deal with anyroad. Nope?

harmless. He could be witty too. Also, a pipe kinked out of his mouth in a manner the ww found comforting. What all this had to do with supplements, God knew.

The ww, at this point, did not herself know God.

When asked his opinion on her appearance one Saturday evening, the ww's dad replied that she did not have a fizzog that would stop a clock ticking. The ww was non-plussed as to whether or not to take this as a compliment.

Sometimes the ww lay her head on a towel in the airing cupboard and left it resting there for up to ten minutes.

And yet nor had it escaped the ww's notice that her two piles of supplements had prospered about the same time as her mom's habit of switching words around had started to become increasingly obvious. In fact, when she thought about it, the ww realised that the second pile had come into existence the same day she had decided to start a dictionary of her mom's slippages (the dictionary consisted of a slip of paper slid beneath the rolling pin in a drawer in the kitchen). The ww, it should probably be noted, was good at keeping track of dates. That's how she was able to correlate the day of the dictionary and the commencement of the second pile. Ever since she'd started her period at what was then considered the precocious age of eleven, the ww's periods had been as regular as clockwork. They were spot on. It was as if she had the moon tucked up in her womb, basically. And because of this reliability, which according to her mom was quite unusual, even though that was how it was supposed to work, wasn't it, because of this the ww could always pin-point the day on which such and such a thing had happened. All she had to do was consider whether or not she'd been on her period at the time and if yes then at what stage of it, whether the blood had been ruby or rusty or pouring or stodgy, etc., and she could narrow the dates down until she nailed it. So it was in this way that she realised that the second supplement pile had been started the same day as the dictionary of slippages.

It was supposed to be tenderly humorous, the dictionary. By fish wire the ww tied two biros through a hole punched in the paper's corner. One biro, a red one, was for writing down the ww's mom's word; the other biro, a blue one, was for entering the translation. It was all in good humour. The ww's mom's thing with words wasn't, at this stage, the overt problem it was on its way to becoming. It wasn't even really a foible. It certainly wasn't chronic. 'Chronic' was yet to acquire its association with something irreversible or inveterate. To the ww, 'chronic' suggested something that had gone on for yonks, but which wasn't necessarily a foible. In this way the universe was chronic. Humanity was chronic. The ww's parents were chronic.

"Time as we know it was invented right here, in this city."

That was what the ww's dad had announced once at supper. Afterwards, the ww had watched the bubbles in his beer rise upwards.

It wasn't as if the ww's mom suddenly started speaking

complete gibberish. That wasn't it at all. It was, to begin with, always easy to comprehend what she was getting at. To begin with it was only the odd word that got swapped. Instead of doing the Hoovering, the ww's mom did the mowing. Instead of putting the kettle on, she put her head on. Instead of asking the ww to place the clean mugs back in the cupboard she asked the ww to put them in the refrigerator (*eigentlich* the ww's mom did *eigentlich* do this herself once: the refrigerator was new, and had made a big impression on her). Instead of asking to be passed the salt, she asked to be passed the elephant. Instead of eating her spaghetti, she ate her alphabet (this one was clearly encouraged by the increased availability at the time of Heinz's Alphabetti Spaghetti, although the ww's mom wasn't eating that particular canned product the day she made the swappage). Often the words that got swapped were the words for the things the ww's mom had temporarily lost. Instead of arriving home exceptionally late from a matinée screening and explaining how she'd misplaced her buzz stub, the ww's mom explained how she'd misplaced her postcard. To the ww's mind, there was a clear connection to be made between her mom's misplacing of things and her replacing of their monikers, words. The one weakness segued into the other. When the ww quizzed her mom about it, the ww's mom answered, while tugging contemplatively on an earlobe, that she had enjoyed learning shorthand in secretarial college, that she had possessed an unusual aptitude for it, and that perhaps that had something to do with it.

The ww wasn't convinced.

But the word thing did get her thinking. It was entirely possible, she now contemplated, that her interest in the supplements that landed with *The Post* on the doormat had more to do with the word 'supplement' than the material objects. The neatly folded pages, the thin, crisp paper, the vomity smell of the inside spreads: all that was so much stuffing. It was possible that it was the word 'supplement', the word alone, for which the ww's collection spoke a strange love. Although this didn't explain the ww's careful stapling of each new supplement that wasn't already stapled (increasingly, some were), an act that was material in nature, it did definitely tally with the dispassionate aspect of her interest. In a way, it was the word 'supplement' alone that the ww was collecting, even though the word 'supplement' wasn't actually present in any of the supplements. All the actual printed inky words within them were nothing more than a distraction, which was why the ww didn't read them.

Anyroad, whether accurate or not, the ww decided to go along with this realisation about the possible significance of the word 'supplement.' She did so by setting out to assemble in her diary as many definitions of it as she could think of.

We have already dwelt briefly on one of these definitions. Let us now return to it. A supplement, we said, is something secondary (it owes its existence to something else, or at the very least always exists in relation to something else) yet at the same time separate (it exists independently of the thing that spawned it). What interested the ww most about this definition, which she was proud to have come up with, was that from a certain perspective it also described what it was to be the child of somebody. A child, too, owed its existence to its parent, but was also, or craved eventually to be, independent of that parent. Of course, a child's extent of independence varied according to how you defined 'independent.' In this respect, the ww made a point of being aware of the fact that, like all humans, she had been born an incompetent imbecile, that compared to babba goats and foals and most other young mammals all human beings were born extremely prematurely, that in contrast to the entire animal kingdom it took humans yonks to learn to walk on their own two legs (this being the case whatever way you looked at it, whether physically, pecuniarily or metaphorically). All this the ww took on board. But what she also pointed out (to the imaginary interlocutor in her brain) was that this was exactly the beauty of her first definition of the word 'supplement.' The element of independence it involved was tempered by the element of relationability it also stated, this being the idea that a supplement was something that always existed in relationship to something other than it. As a child of somebody, existence wasn't something you *had*, so much as something you had inherited.

At this point in her workings the ww had scowled at the illegibility of her handwriting, blown a raspberry, and tucked her diary under her mattress. Her wardrobe was echoing the tap-tapping of her dad's knuckles on the wall of her parents' bedroom, which adjoined the ww's room on the opposite side of the airing cupboard. That night the ww dreamed vividly about her dad's accident, the one to do with the tower block. In her dream it was this more recent accident that had caused her dad the loss of his left leg, and not whatever it was that had *eigentlich* caused it. The ww didn't know the details of the tower block accident, which was probably why she dreamt about it so often.

The house the ww grew up in was bigger than it needed to be. There was a spare room far more spacious than the ww's, but the ww never got around to moving into it. The ww's dad often wondered aloud at what the three of them were doing rattling round a house 'this size', an observation which, upon his retirement, he consciously or otherwise made a point of making literal.

Anyroad. Another definition of 'supplement' that the ww came up with was this: a supplement completes something that is not in itself incomplete. Now, the ww realised that this definition sounded very much like a paradox. But it was a paradox that anybody could understand if they put their head to it. For example, it was not unusual for two lovers, or even twins if they were close enough, to talk as though each one completed the other. This was still the case even though, obviously, each individual operated as a complete system in terms of bodily functions, nervous system, etc. Also, you just had to think of the way in which any money earned by a housewife in a part-time job or whatever was classed as a 'supplement' to her husband's income. At this the ww huffed internally, though at the same she recognised it as a useful illustration of her point about a supplement being something that completes something which is not incomplete. The ww knew that her mom, like her dad, worked in Eden when she was younger, but that she'd given up her job to care for the ww. That was what moms did. They gave up for their children. And when the ww had turned approximately seven years old, the ww's mom had taken a new job three mornings a week as a receptionist in an optician's: she hated it compared to her old work, but did it to supplement the ww's dad's income.

After a while the ww gave up compiling definitions. Their abstract clarity, she suspected, was only increasing her confusion about the two piles in her boxy bedroom. Though the definitions were seductive, they were not very helpful. They were like a meaningful wink the ww didn't know the meaning of. They mostly just made her forget why she was coming up with them in the first place. And the ww also sensed that things were far, far messier than any single definition could cope with. A definition of the kind she'd been coming up with might look like it had cut a direct line between *a* and *b*, and in a sense it had done, but in doing so, in cutting that line, it had also caused a kind of destruction, the nature of which the ww couldn't quite put her finger on. The ww realised that the delight she took in these definitions was in itself in danger of becoming a fresh foible. Her mom's word thing amused her greatly, but it also made her nervous and alert to her own tendencies. Once, during a swimming lesson, the ww had obeyed an instruction to dive into the water and do five strokes whilst still underwater by diving into the water and whilst still underwater doing one stroke of breaststroke, one spasm of doggy paddle, one stroke of front crawl (which turned out much like the spasm of doggy paddle) and then, upon attempting to roll over and do an underwater stroke of backstroke, swallowing a gallon of chlorinated water and almost drowning.

The one thing the ww never put her finger near was this: it never occurred to the ww that her collection of supplements might not have had anything whatsoever to do with anything already around her. That is, it never occurred to the ww that she might be acting *now* in relation to something that was *yet to happen*, that she was building the piles in preparation for something that was still to come into being, not because of something that already existed (like her dad's percussive perambulations or her mom's inadvertent wordplay) and which was invisibly bothering the ww (that people were invisibly bothered by things was not something the ww had needed the supplement about psychoanalysis to teach her).

Noah didn't build an ark because his dad died at sea, did he?

What the ww was not accounting for, which you would have thought her study of the psychoanalysis supplement might have begun to teach her, was that the recesses of the mind, those folds of it responsible for idiosyncratic ticks and foibles, are totally ignorant of time as we know it. That is, they do not know what time is. Time — or at least straight-up, industrial time, the kind of time the ww's dad was attempting to talk about that one time at supper— is to those grey kinks irrelevant. Had the ww been at all interested in religion at this point (as with so many converts, the ww vociferously hated anything vaguely religious up until the moment of her conversion, which is, anyroad, something that occurred later, a good while after the momentous realisation associated with the portable stapler) — had the ww been more interested in the Biblical texts and their literary derivatives she might have been wiser, about time. When Adam and Eve leave the Garden of Eden, the world they are entering is — what? The world is *all before them*. All before them. There already. But also *yet to come into existence*. Been there, done that, but what you've been to and done is still to happen. There and back to see where it is.

Some people spend their whole lives saying sorry for something they haven't done yet.

A few more words about the ww's environment. The ww and her parents lived, as mentioned, in a cottage, albeit a big cottage. It was situated amongst a number of other cottages, all built within five years of one another, or thereabouts. A lot of the cottages were semi-detached, others were terraced, though the terraced ones looked nothing like the tunnelbacks that ran in rigid lines a short walk away. For the idea behind the area in which the ww and her parents lived was that it should be attached to the city yet simultaneously feel completely different to it: the idea was that their area should feel, if not exactly villagey, then approximately rural. There were many trees and much foliage, though not all of this was fully developed. The ww's house had three undulations of grass in front of it. The middle undulation was studded with an apple tree. The apples were inedible raw but the ww's mom nonetheless collected those of the fallen that were not squashed and pussy and then used these apples for cooking. At the bottom of the road, which was never referred to as a street, ever, there was an island, and in the island a greengrocer's, and behind the greengrocer's some tennis courts. To live in one of the cottages you had to rent a house from the association of tenants. None of the cottages had been bomb-damaged. The ww's dad, the ww sensed, didn't much like living where they did but never stated so explicitly. From her parents' window you had a view of pitched brown roofs and in the distance, about two miles away, two new tower blocks poking the firmament. The ww suspected that her dad enjoyed the incongruity of the tower blocks, which were made out of concrete. The two tower blocks being basically two fingers up at the pastoral wiggle that lay before them.

The ww was in the habit of swallowing four aspirins daily, two in the mornings and two before sleeping. This obviously had nothing to do with the piles of supplements in her bedroom.

Possibly she would eventually be able to sell her

collection at   some car-boot sale. It was possible that in the future the supplements would be valuable to someone. They were, after all, almost immaculate.

The ww wasn't sure whether the accident that had led to her dad's early retirement had happened in one of the tower blocks visible from her parent's window. She'd never asked.

Once, at supper, the ww's mom told a story about the ww's granddad. The story was one the ww's granddad had himself told. In it, the ww's granddad went to visit a friend with whom he enjoyed the occasional whiskey. Over whiskey and cashew nuts the friend described to the ww's granddad the house he would like to build one day. The house was to have a pitched roof and be an ordinary brick house, with the exception that all the rooms would be not hollow, but solid: the brick house would be bricked-up entirely. That was the house this friend of the ww's granddad wished to build one day.

Sadness (the ww wrote in her diary) is not tears. Sadness is all the tears that over the years are *not* cried.

Can you believe it, the ww's granddad died in a cemetery.

The well incident was such a strange thing. In retrospect it was even stranger that it happened the day before the ww discovered her birth certificate. The cottage in which the ww lived with her parents was not supposed to have a well in its yard. It didn't even have a yard, the cottage; it had a back garden, which unlike the undulating front garden was flat and treeless, though very flowery. The well must have belonged to whatever house had existed before the cottage was built, which in itself was something the ww had to wind her head around. That it was probable that rigid rows of tunnelbacks similar to the ones a short walk away had once ruled lines across the same stretch of earth where the cottages now stood, this seemed strange and inverted. But it was probably, after all, why there was a well in the garden. The ww and her parents had had no idea the well existed until one sunny mid-morning the ww's mom stepped out to peg the bedsheets and stepped into a cylindrical chasm. What was amazing was that the ww's mom broke nothing. The absolutely worst thing, according to her account, was that the neighbours' cat had followed her into the cylindrical chasm (the ww's mom hadn't realised it was a well till later). This was awful, because the ww's mom hated cats and anything both furry and animate and couldn't stand being close to a living example of one, let alone trapped in a well with one. The ww's mom yelled and yelled but the ww's dad was so busy roaming through the rooms and stairwells of the cottage, tapping at the walls and so on, that he heard nothing. It was the ww who eventually realised that her mom was missing, and who let down the wooden ladder.

The next day the ww heard *The Post* slap the porch step with a pitch that screamed: *supplement*. In the new quiet of the cottage — that day her dad had got up and gone straight outside to gaze into the well cavity — the ww heard the sound very distinctly. And it was after whipping the supplement out of its swaddling and tossing the newspaper proper onto a sidetable in the frilly living room that the ww ran up to her parents' bedroom where in the bottom drawer of her mom's vanity chest, next to foam rollers, the familial portable stapler was kept. And when, inexplicably, the stapler was not where it should have been and so the ww pulled open the penultimate drawer and fished around for it — it was then, with the supplement still gripped in her hand, that the ww came across her birth certificate.

Afterwards, the ww would not consciously associate this momentous discovery with the onset of her interest in the building of the inner ring road. But it was nonetheless the case that the supplement she was holding when she happened across her birth certificate was the same supplement that described the Corporation's plans for a brand new city, a city in which people did not perambulate or take mechanically-enhanced bicycle rides or even catch the tram or the buzz, a city to be redefined by roads for motorcars, and, to begin with, by one road in particular: the inner ring road, otherwise known as the A4400.

CONVALESCENCE

B24

In y6, the world fell over. Worlds End was a bad place to be, and I did not want to go anymore. St. John, who was my father, who had not been there when we had given Watt his chocolate box burial, who collected me from school when my mom was working at NEXT, a clothes shop with a name that was the same as the word forever yelled by the dinner ladies at Worlds End — St. John was the one who told me that the fall was *always happening*. I didn't tell him that whenever I saw someone fall over it made me laugh so hard my heart shook. I didn't tell him anything about the game of WOLF and the girl's knickers and the wall I had been made to stand against by the angry Tis'er. Of how my knees had thrilled when the Tis'er told me I could move and I couldn't, I said nothing. Instead, I said I couldn't understand how one thing that had happened once could at the same time always be happening.

I couldn't understand it, so St. John suggested I imagine a time machine combined with a time bomb. I couldn't, so he suggested I imagine a time *capsule* buried deep in the earth then dug up again each day, forever, its contents closely peered at, never altered.

There was a programme I used to watch on TV about a time machine built by the Romans. The machine had been concealed in mud for centuries. Two boys about my age — or they could have been a fraction older than me — these two boys had discovered the time machine and got it working again. The machine was futuristic in a weird way. I didn't think it looked very Roman. In my mind, 'Roman' signified people dressed up in elaborately folded togas, apples, an appreciation of classical combat derived from the TV show *Gladiators*, and Julius Caesar shouting "I came, I saw, I conquered" (and not in Latin). Add to this *tableau* a coin washed in Coca Cola, dead straight roads, a rude statue, and bingo: welcome to the Roman Empire according to Rita.

By this reckoning the time machine discovered by the boys did not look Roman at all. It seemed to me more likely to be a machine that someone from still another period in history had constructed, travelled to the time of the Roman Empire with, and then, after falling in love with togas, or rude statues, abandoned. The Romans had then stumbled upon the machine whilst out strolling, munching apples. Having figured out its function, they themselves had eventually used the machine to zoom around discovering things from *their* future, *the* future obviously being in reality a relative entity, since, in the grand scheme of things, what for one person is still to happen is for another person already over and done with. It was possible that the non-Roman origin of the time machine was implicit in the TV programme's backstory. If so I didn't notice. I was too busy considering that if the Romans had stolen their best ideas not from the Greeks (this is what St. John had told me they had done) but from their future, then, in the grand scheme of things, the past had been built out of the future and the future was not the future and the present was all over the place.

I loved that TV programme. It was on at big hand E little hand N every Friday. I never cared what happened in it. Nothing new ever happened in it. It was always the same adventure enacted slightly differently every episode. The concluding section of each episode was spent in a panicked rush to return to the present, with the two boys inevitably finding themselves stuck in some 'wrong' future that it had then fallen upon them to 'correct', which they usually decided to do by going back in time then fast-forwarding again to check everything had turned out OK. The fact that they possessed a time machine and could return to the present at a push of a button — this basic fact never seemed to occur either to the boys or to the programme's makers. I can't say it occurred to me. It didn't matter. It wasn't the point. It was enough just to admire all the machine's levers and buttons. Its frame was strangely mammalian.

I used to think about where the machine was when it wasn't anywhere, when it was traveling along cosmic slip roads or stalled at a system interchange between two destinations. The programme was on after the cartoons had ended (at which point the chirruping presenter had four minutes to introduce what was coming on next), and I ate an apple whenever I watched it. I would sit with my knees bent to my chin, chomping, transfixed.

It was one of the few programmes the twins tolerated watching with me when they were living with us, which was every weekend from Friday after school to Sunday evening. The twins were non-identical. They didn't *stay* with us. They *lived* with us, but not all of the time. Usually they snorted at my choice of TV programme and either turned the TV off or forced me to crouch behind the sofa, so that they could watch whatever they wanted to without getting into trouble for letting me watch with them. I refused, once, to budge, and my punishment was to stand one-legged on a chair, knickers down, bum to the window, for the duration of their preferred programme. They said all the world had seen me, and even though I knew this was impossible, I believed them.

The Roman time machine stopped flying the spring before y6 began. I forgot about it over the course of the summer and only remembered it again when St. John started talking about time-machines combined with time-bombs. The two boys had discovered the machine dumped in a ditch somewhere, covered in mud, like a time capsule. I sometimes wondered where the Romans who had abandoned it had got to, whether they had remained in the present they had landed in and gone into the future with that present, in time with it. When I posed this question to the twins they groaned and declared that their mom was prettier than my mom.

I had barely even considered that their mom existed.

~

'Invisibility is as key to the road's success as visibility. For motorists, the road, its placement and its purpose, must be self-evident and eminently legible. Its uniqueness of function should be immediately apparent, something that it is hoped will be achieved by the road's redness (the inner ring road is to be painted red). To the non-motorist, on the other hand, the road should remain inaccessible: not only should physical obstacles be placed in the way of anybody attempting to cross it, but the road itself must function to block its perception by the pedestrian. That is, the road's shapes and signs, whilst clearly perceivable to the motorist, should for the non-motorist be so alien as to be unrecognisable. Of course, once the road is rushing with vehicles, its noise and its density will do much to contribute to the discouragement of pedestrians. The creation of subways is also significant. But the importance of building invisibility into the road's design — so that the road becomes nothing but a blot in the pedestrian's consciousness — should not be underestimated. In short, this is a road that the pedestrian must not think about stepping onto.'

Adapted from a draft of a paper dictated by Manzino to the bab; scored by the bab in shorthand; deposited in a drawer; never returned to.

~

PRECIPITATION

BI IBB

It seems wrong, somehow, to doodle in shorthand. As shorthand is a system constructed for quickness, economy and efficiency, it seems wrong to toss a curl and dot of it into the corner of a newspaper when someone is talking about something boring, or when your daydreams have got the better of you and you have sent your own self to Coventry, i.e. submerged yourself in silence. It seems wrong to doodle in shorthand on the wall of a toilet cubicle, even if you are stuck in that toilet. That, though, is what the bab does. That is what the bab is doing right now. The bab is doodling in shorthand on the wall of a toilet in Eden.

According to B3, the bab getting stuck in the toilet is becoming something of an Eden ritual. That it always seems to happen on Tuesday afternoons — the same day the bab trots out for a lunch date with her father, then trots back into the office all ashen and shrivelled — this is not something that has escaped B3's notice. As B3 would himself point out, B3 notices things like that. He has greedy eyes and big ones. Each time the bab gets stuck, B3 makes a consequential mark on his calendar. The bab contends that her getting stuck is nothing more than her stupidly forgetting that the sliding bolt on the toilet door at the end of the row in 'the ladies' is a particularly sticky bolt, and that if you shove it a fraction too far, it jams. The metal gets trapped and so does the bab. After a few attempts it's usually possible to ease the bolt back out, but this has to be done gradually, with patience. It's no use panicking. It's no use ruining a blouse by using the fabric to give friction to your grip on the bolt. Each attempt to release the dinky bullet needs to be done with the utmost carefulness and only an ambivalent glimmer of hope. Stay casual, calm. If you hope too much, the bolt will know. This is what the bab thinks. The quiver of your fingers will quiver into it and *it* — the dinky bullet — will suck up the quivers and start panicking too.

"Take your time now."

"Breathe."

"Not too quickly now."

"Breathe."

"Don't panic."

"Breathe."

"And relax."

These are the words the bab finds herself saying to herself when she gets stuck in the bog, which is how the *other* would describe what tends to happen to the bab on Tuesday afternoons. In the minutes between attempts at the bolt, she tilts her neck, slaps down the toilet seat, rearranges her undergarments so as to perch comfortably, extracts a pencil from behind an earflap, doodles.

The bab doodles in shorthand.

The walls in the toilet are greyish white. The porcelain

toilet bowl is greyish white, too. Apart from the toilet lid and the toilet chain everything in the toilet cubicle is some shade of greyish white. And when you stare at grey walls for long enough, the walls stop being blank planes, as walls painted one colour customarily are, and instead reveal their dimples, their indented squirms and raised dots. This has the consequence that getting stuck in the cubicle at the end of the row in 'the ladies' can make the bab feel as if she is stuck inside a brain. The dimples and ridges and wrinkles made by the paint become somehow like thoughts. When peered at for long enough, the dimples and ridges and wrinkles on the walls remind the bab of thoughts. In those minutes between attempts on the bolt, she forgets all about her work on the map, about the buggy eyes of B3, about the plan she is helping Manzino to plot ('neither an urban motorway, nor principally a traffic street, nor a shopping thoroughfare'). The bab forgets all about these sorts of things (she forgets the pumice stone and the piece of chalk; she even forgets the bombs) and writes back to the thoughts on the wall.

The bab writes back in shorthand.

She loves shorthand. For as long as she has known its inscriptions, she has loved shorthand. She picked it up extremely easily, much more easily than the girls who were on her training course with her. They stuck their thumbs in their gobs and complained about the obscurity. The bab stuck her stiletto heels into the classroom floor and got on with it. The training course took place in a room in the Central Library not far from Eden, where the floor was already well-punctured with stiletto studs, so the bab didn't bother to take her shoes off during lessons. The bab just stuck her heels in and got on with the learning of shorthand.

She got on with shorthand very well. The cover of the 'reader' she graduated to once she'd mastered the basics announced itself as an edition for a 'new era' —

PITMAN'S SHORTHAND NEW ERA EDITION
GRADED LITERARY SHORTHAND READER
A SERIES OF NARRATIVE EXERCISES FOR USE IN
THEORY AND SPEED CLASSES

— and that, somehow, was exactly what the bab felt about what was going on in the dingy classroom in which she and the other girls were taught: shorthand was a revelation, *a new era*. The bab had been good at algebra at school but had not really seen the point of it. According to a decision her mom had made, back when Doug was yet to make his patriarchal intervention, the bab was going to become a Tis'er in an infant school, and Tis'ers in infant school didn't need to know algebra, or at least not much of it. Algebra certainly had an abstract beauty, but shorthand had a way of wafting across a page far more gracefully. The bab nibbled the rubbers off many a pencil during the six months of the training course, she was so eager to get on with it.

The strokes come to her now as quickly as words written

with regular characters. They come even quicker. Lines and dashes. Curves. Horizontal bars. Vertical slashes. Arcs rolling on their bottoms. Loops and hooks, circles and semi-circles, ticks and dots, stitches. The way all these marks converge in a kind of precise gymnastics pleases the bab the immeasurably. It wouldn't be going too far to say that it thrills her. To begin with she set about assiduously working through the tasks the instructor set them in class, copying out the patterns slowly, tracing a bend or squiggle or semi-circle repeatedly until it was perfect. The bab became more accomplished with each task they were given. Then the instructor, a bouncy, perennially bedraggled woman, picked up on the bab's eagerness and nurtured it as she had nurtured each of her chubby babbas: she fed the bab more and more until the bab was bursting. For some reason grotesquely offended by this enthusiasm for something so difficult, the girl the bab sat next to started to snarl at the bab in a manner not at all pleasant. Eyes squeezed to slits, she practically hissed at her. After a nod of a neat little nose and a tart, sarcastic greeting, she would snub the bab for the two girls who sat at the table behind. The three of them would then chat about their weekends until the instructor shuffled, wet-haired when it wasn't even raining, through the door beside the blackboard. At that point the girls' tongues would shush, become slithery:

"Gawd, here comes fatso."

"Fatso and her army of stickmen."

"Here's boiled egg with her skinny soldiers."

Those were the sort of cruelties the girls sniggered and got lipstick stuck on their teeth about. The bab, meanwhile, was getting on incredibly well. The shorthand exercises got easier and easier. The exercises stopped looking like stickmen doing cartwheels and instead started shuddering with meaning. In a snap, the bab began to be able to read a paragraph of simple shorthand. The bab could now read a paragraph of shorthand in a snap. It was easy. It was brilliant. To take down what the instructor dictated was tougher, and was a skill that took longer to master, and wasn't made any easier by the girls' constant sniggering, but the bab tried hard and made good progress. Her concentration improved. Her brain hiccupped drunkenly with each new dart or flap she learnt. The stitches and kisses signified something. The stickmen danced.

The girls were told always to use pencils for shorthand. It was too messy to use pen nibs and ink. The bab understood this instinctively.

The stickmen danced.

Then at the end of one of the sessions, the instructor held the bab back. The rest of the girls trooped out to their next activity, pulling fizzogs. The shorthand lessons were only one element in a week of various secretarial pursuits. The bab didn't mind typing, which they practiced to loud music that came from a gramophone at the front of the classroom. Nor did she mind learning the ins and outs of writing memos, nor even, really, the class they called 'comportment', which was all about walking around with a pile of books on your head.

The bab did not mind these activities. She quite liked them. But shorthand was her true love.

Ignorant of the silent jeers behind her back, her back still damp from the wet hair that fell there, the instructor had come shuffling over to the bab with a small blue book in her puddingy hand.

"Here."

"What is it?"

"*Alice's Adventures in Wonderland* by Lewis Carroll."

The bab had been confused at first, unable to grasp the point of the book being given her. Then she peered at its spine, gasped, glanced shyly at the instructor.

"In shorthand?"

The instructor's considerable jaw had dropped like a bomb.

"Of course, dear."

The bab peered again at the book, opened its first pages. There on the inside cover was the instructor's name.

"Translated by you! Is 'translated' the right word?"

The instructor nodded briskly, embarrassed.

"Yes. It's good practice, and pleasant. Here, there's also this."

That was when the instructor had presented the bab with the 'new era' edition of the *Graded Literary Shorthand Reader*. On her way home by tram to 140 Armoury Road — all this being before the bab moved out of her parent's boarding house — she turned through the book's pages solemnly.

There were ten excerpts in all, including one from *Robinson Crusoe* by Daniel Defoe, one from *Treasure Island* by Robert Louis Stevenson, one from *Hansel and Grethel* by Grimm, one from *The Silent Judge* by someone called Maxwell Crooks, one from *Clarissa Harlowe, or the History of a Young Lady* by Samuel Richardson, and one from *Tristram Shandy* by Lawrence Sterne. Then there was an excerpt from the *Thoughts and Theories* of I. J. Pitman. The bab presumed that this Pitman was the same Pitman responsible for the shorthand forms she was currently being taught, and so she was very intrigued to know whether these thoughts and theories of his had been composed in his system of shorthand in the first place, or whether they too had been written regularly and then only later transposed or translated, or whatever was the right word.

As the tram stammered and panted its way down from Colmore Row along Livery Street, the bab ignored the random body parts bouncing off her own and instead dug her head into *Tristram*, into Pitman's *Thoughts and Theories*. The excerpt from *Robinson Crusoe* began with a vertical line dotted at the top on the left hand side, an upside down arch hooked at the right with one thick stumpy leg sticking out, an isolated spot, and a bent dash dotted on the bottom right. The bab had never read anything by Daniel Defoe before. As the tram stammered on past flanks of red buildings runny with soot, collecting more body parts at every stop, the bab completed a paragraph by Samuel Richardson. The bab had never read anything by Richardson before. Apart from those in the boarders' own rooms, there weren't many books in the house on Armoury Road. Her mom never read anything but cookbooks. Doug preferred the movies.

The two other excerpts in the 'reader' were both non-fictional. The bab was put off one of them because the 'text' in question contained many numbers, which the bab eventually realised were dates. The dates were written ordinarily, as digits, so that in the midst of a smooth run of curls etc. there would suddenly appear an '1832', or an '1848', or an '1905.' Though she did grasp the fact that these kind of numbers are in themselves a form of shorthand (as opposed to numbers that are written out in word form) and that it would therefore be daft to invent even shorter forms for them, the bab nonetheless felt a strange distaste, seeing them there on the page. They looked so crude compared to shorthand proper.

The bab's head was still bent into the shorthand 'reader' when she stepped off the tram at the top of the hill, where a road of older buildings swept round to meet a dip of tunnelbacks. The boarding house at 140 was one of the big old buildings; what once must have been imposing, perpendicular and robust was now shabby, slouched. The roofs of the tunnelbacks dived down the hill in staggered folds. The roofs of the big old buildings sagged, grimaced, got shoved to the side by more tunnelbacks. The roads of tunnelbacks raced, striped and dashed. The rolling hills budged their lines into arcs. The sun was a stitch of yellow blinking behind a cloud. The bab saw shorthand in everything now: stepping down off the tram and raising her eyes from the 'reader', she saw not roofs and chimneys but ticks and darts, read them, heard what the roads and houses were muttering.

The bab began to hear structures muttering everywhere. Lamp-posts, cables, washing lines: in these the bab saw flashes of Pitman's stickmen, read them, heard what they muttered.

Olsy always hated it when she caught the bab aimlessly gazing. Olsy, as usual, was on her way out somewhere. Her hair dark apart from one thick shock of outrageous blonde, she passed the bab coming up the hill, stuck out her tongue, waltzed off. As usual, Olsy waltzed off. 'There she goes again, jettin' like a crow in the gutter', is what the *other* would say of Olsy's strut.

After that, the bab got faster and faster at shorthand. After *Tristram* and *Crusoe* — all read as the tram stammered back and forth past red buildings runny with soot, or as the bab stepped through streets everywhere carved into consonants and vowels — after that it became as easy for her to take notes in shorthand as it was for her to read shorthand. The instructor dictated excerpts from *Middlemarch* by George Eliot; the bab made quick sharp shapes. The instructor dictated segments of a translation of *Anna Karenina*; the bab inscribed Anna's life on her page. Able to do the others' work for them should they prefer not to do it themselves, the bab became immensely popular amongst the girls on her course. The girl she shared her table with grew kind wide eyes and snubbed the two girls who sat at the table behind. Now she elbowed the bab intimately, even sharpened the bab's blunt pencils.

"Aren't those two *so* silly?"

"Here yo go, bab. Have a nice sharp one."

So pleased to have nurtured such a talent, the instructor positively blushed at the bab's perfect scores. The six-month course came to an end. The bab aced the tests at her interview with the City Council, started work, celebrated a century of *incorporation* in the Grand Hotel on Colmore Row, danced badly with Manzino in the Grand's marblecake ballroom, drank too much punch, went off to Livery Street with the *other*, then a clerk in the Planning Department in Eden, soon to become Surveyor for Area Code B19, the area where the bab's parents ran their boarding house on Armoury Road.

Frank, the bab's younger brother, was still at home then. A schoolboy, keen on art. A wonderful dancer. Always making brick walls, i.e. always gobbling his food.

Olsy became fabulouser and fabulouser. Olsy was always on her way out somewhere. Olsy savaged the bab's fashion sense constantly. In return the bab loved her increasingly savagely, even though, or possibly because, Olsy no longer wanted the bab in the room when she was snogging somebody.

The bab meanwhile did well at work, was one day asked by Manzino to take a memo, impressed him with her speediness and conversational knowledge of *Robinson Crusoe*, became Manzino's personal secretary, saved enough of her wages to move out of the boarding house at 140 Armoury

Road.

Olsy was still on her way out somewhere, still hated it when she caught the bab aimlessly gazing. Through her hair sped a shock of blonde.

The *other* left to fight in fields. Frank was soon to follow.

The bab began to get the feeling that she was putting the world off until the world stopped putting her off. The bab wanted to tell her older sister a secret, but what that secret was, she wasn't sure. The bab did have the feeling that the secret had something to do with how she felt about shorthand, and that the way she felt about shorthand had something to do with Olsy no longer wanting her in the room when she was snogging boarders, and that it wasn't Olsy whom this eviction made the bab envious of, but the boarders, and that this fierce envy the bab felt definitely contributed to the urge to draw shorthand inscriptions on the walls of toilet cubicles — but still, she wasn't sure. It was interesting that despite her missing him terribly, the *other* never featured in the bab's privy inscriptions.

The bombs started falling. The bab felt sort of fallen herself. The bab turned up to work one day and saw a map spread out before her. Manzino pointed to the map, spoke to her softly but thoroughly, and the map became hers. The map became her work. Steadied by pumice stone, bag of sand, and piece of chalk, it was there, waiting for her, each time she stepped through the Enquiry Office door. A queue of fizzogs as long as Livery Street crept around Eden, told the bab their horrid stories. The bab transformed the stories into red and black circles of altering circumference, pillowed her skull with foam sausages, ignored B3's terrible jokes and bulgy eyes, which were also, she had recently noted, starting to grow bushy brows.

The days continued. So did the bombs.

Then all of a sudden Olsy was not on her way out somewhere anymore: she was gone. At least with Frank and the *other*, the bab had known where to. The *other* had not wanted to go.

Doug's drinking worsened. The bab's mom did nothing but cook all day, barely eating anything herself. The boarding house rooms, now almost emptied, sucked on the odours coming from the overflowing stove.

One early afternoon, over tea and rolls in the ODEON restaurant, at around big hand O little hand a fraction past E, Doug asked the bab to find out what was up with Olsy. He had not asked in so many words. That was not Doug's way. But the bab had understood. For two weeks she had manipulated her position as Humphrey B. Manzino's personal secretary to make telephone calls to landlords in B19, in B17, in B6, even in the Corporation estates of B24, at that point still hardly populated. The landlords answered, their throats reluctant and disrupted at first, then, when the bab told them where it was that she worked, cooing, undulatory, very accommodating. The bab explained that she was calling to speak to a woman for whom the Corporation's Housing Office had found a new house, but that they had lost track of the woman unfortunately and that perhaps she was now boarding with that very landlord in B19, or B6, or B24? Eventually, after many snotty tuts from B3 and then many telephone calls made after working hours, when B3 and B17 and even Manzino, if he wasn't sleeping in his office, had gone, when the bab could send the numbers on the dial spinning round without B3 asking whom exactly she was telephoning now — eventually she found her.

So now the bab writes in shorthand on the walls of Eden's toilets on Tuesday afternoons. Olsy: a forward bulging upright arc. Olsy: a forward bulging upright arc, an end bracket, a paunch, a big old ear, a zero sliced down the middle.

The bab sighs gently. Getting up from the toilet lid, she slides the pencil back behind an ear, wipes her hands as well as she can on a crinkle of toilet roll, then has another go at the bolt. The bab has been stuck in the cubicle for approximately ten minutes. This is her second attempt to push the bolt free.

"Take your time."

"Breathe."

"Not too quickly now."

"Breathe."

But the bolt's silver nubbin slips from her fingers with the first thrust. The bab gazes at it aimlessly, then sits back down. The piece of toilet roll she still holds has a texture not dissimilar to a scrunch of elephant-sized tracing paper blithely tossed by B3 in the bin.

The bab slides the pencil back out from behind an ear, writes an upright arc expanding to the right with a hook at the top on the left.

The bab hasn't heard from the *other* in yonks.

This morning, before the bab went out to meet Doug, a wiry woman with one glass eye came into the Enquiry Office to report a bomb. The bomb had splat straight into the house the glass eye shared with her daughter and her daughter's two daughters and baby son. There was a husband too, but he was AWOL. They'd heard nothing from him nor of him. As the joggling glass eye informed the bab (the bab hadn't been able to see anything but a glass eye joggling), there had been no envelopes and no telegram. As far as the glass eye was concerned, this was all for the good. The husband had been useless: beery, skinny, politically odd (the glass eye was always coming across nonsensical slogans printed on leaflets or scribbled by the husband in the margin of some silly book), and worst of all (so the glass eye said, insinuatingly, in a way that made the bab feel very cold towards the cold ogle joggling before her) not even *from* hereabouts. The glass eye had always suspected her daughter's husband would eventually run off. The glass eye, according to the glass eye, was beady, sharp, always wiping her own daughter's eye (i.e. seeing what her daughter failed to see for herself). The bab, accustomed now to the narrative elaborations of her terrible visitors, wrapped her palm around the pumice stone, smoothed the map with her other hand, wished she would be shocked by what was still to come. Two desks down, B3 picked his nose. B15 pinched the skin on his hands. The bomb, the glass eye reported, had broken the sky, dazzled the dark, slammed all the doors, smacked into the strip of turf between the house and the metal shelter the husband had built before he'd gone. The glass eye had been visiting her sister and had taken with her, thanks be to God, her daughter's son. She had seen the sky ignite and sizzle, and out of habit, out of habit alone, she'd made a wish on a falling star. The next morning the glass eye returned from her sister's (who was a wonderful cook) to find two bodies buried in twinkling earth. The earth was twinkling, she eventually realised, because the shards of the broken windows had glittered the mud. The third body, which had flown two garden fences and one brick wall, was discovered by the postman slumped up against a postbox. It wasn't a body he had found so much as body *parts*: one leg and a trunk folded up against the postbox and one arm draped voluptuously across the postbox's convex top.

At that, the bab had laughed.

The laugh came grimly up from her stomach through her gullet into her mouth. She had had no choice but to let it come out. It hurt. It burned right through her. B3 stopped picking his nose and put down his book. The glass eye stopped joggling and set its glassiness straight upon the bab. Ten thousand pins dropped from the Enquiry Office's ceiling and each one stuck its point into the bab. The room shrivelled, boomed. The glass eye still set upon her, the bab straightened her blouse, quickly asked for the road and the postcode and went to pencil in a circle on the map. But when she came to the spot, she couldn't: the thin strip of turf the glass eye was pointing to was already smothered by a swarm of blobs. The bab's own eyeballs fizzed in their sockets. Her heels dug new holes in the Enquiry Office floor. It was as if the bap's map had foretold the future. It was as if the map had brought the future into existence. It was as if the bab's map was a magic ball and the bab herself was that fortune teller she had once visited with Olsy, the one from whom Olsy had got the idea of the thick shock of blonde. The bab's map was a magic ball. The bab's map was a bomb. And now the magic ball had shattered, blown up.

What was it in the glass eye's story that had made the bab laugh? The bit about the body parts, the trunk and the leg and the voluptuous arm? Was it funny, that they had been found there by the postbox, as if somebody had tried to post them? Or was it the 'voluptuous' arm that had made the bab laugh? Why had the glass eye described her daughter's severed limb as 'voluptuous'? Had she said that at all? Was the bab making it up? Had that not been very pretty, the bit about the twinkling earth? What was the bab *thinking*, thinking that?

After a while the glass eye had rolled slowly out through the Enquiry Office doors, revolving once as it bumped over the sill and giving the bab a final chastising look. The bab had undug her heels and straightened her blouse. B3 resumed his chirruping; on his desk was an oval plate of Manzino's fig rolls. B17 looked straight ahead, then after a while unwrapped his first spam sarnie of the day. The bab glanced at her watch and went off to the ODEON restaurant to get her tea and to meet, as usual, Doug.

And now the bab is yanking at the bolt in the cubicle at the end of the row in the 'ladies.' Except her hands are nowhere near the bolt. Her hands are quite still by her side: it's her mind that's yanking, yanking, and it's also her mind that is making her stay put inside the cubicle's walls. Her mind likes it in there. The cubicle is one unit of space, and that is what the bab's mind would like to be too. The cubicle doesn't contract and expand and contract. Sure, it smells slightly, but it doesn't shrivel and boom. It doesn't gobble space up like all the circles do on her map. The mess of many fried eggs that her map started out as — that was nothing, the bab realises now. Now her map is one big belching *amoeba* of suckers, sucking up space, a globular cluster belching destruction. The destruction of the past and the destruction of the future. The toilet cubicle is concise, compact, and that is what the bab's mind wants to be too. Concise, compact, with amenable walls and a silvery bolt. The bab does not want to go back to her steel-legged desk in the Enquiry Office and sink her fingers into its leather-spread top, bear the skin on B17's hands and not throw the pumice stone at B3. Now the bab does not want to go back to her map at all.

The bab has had enough. Olsy was right not to like it when she saw the bab aimlessly gazing.

The bab feels really confused.

The bab cannot bear to tell Doug that Olsy is rooming in Livery Street, of all places, and that when the bab found her she was about to explode. A bombshell, a babba, babba boom.

For all its writhing arcs and hoops, shorthand, in the bab's mind, shares something of the compact solitude the bab finds in this toilet cubicle. An upright stroke completing a hook with a diagonal stroke going upwards to the right: what is that, but a thought securely bolted with a silvery bullet? A thought that cannot spread into anything else. Or is B3 right about the significance of these Tuesday afternoons? At first, the bab's love of shorthand had nothing to do with anything at all. It was simple, straightforward. The bab felt at home in shorthand from the off. The little lines dazzled her, sure, but that was partly because it was so astonishing how at ease she felt with them from the off. But then why did she fall in love to begin with at all? Why does anyone fall for anything? Who would be so stupid as to make a wish upon a falling star *now*?

The bab feels confused. Her pencil expertly shimmies over the ridges and pimples in the wall. Lit badly by one bare bulb, the walls of the toilet cubicle at the end of the row in 'the ladies' are almost completely covered: the shorthand stickmen dance manically, stitching, scooping. What B3 would say if ever he snuck into 'the ladies' and saw them, the bab doesn't know. After a morning drawing perfect circles on her map (circles of destruction, circles of nothingness) it's a relief, to come in here. The bab likes to get stuck in the toilet. That's all.

REDEVELOPMENT

B2

So now the ww sits on a padded seat in the Central Library, sweating it out. The seats beside hers are empty. Two small books, two notebooks, the emptied contents of a polka-dot pencil case, the by-now-infamous portable stapler — the ww's stuff is sprawled all across the spare deskspace. The ww would like to be a tidy worker, but she isn't, she's very messy. The metal shade overhanging the section of desk that *is* hers contains a bulb the ww has switched on despite there already being tons of sun coming in through the windows. The bulb isn't properly working, even. It sobs small surges of electricity then crackles off, then beams back on again, crackles off, comes back on again. The ww is content to let it do this. It helps her think somehow. Thinking is thoughtlessness tossed back on itself. The lamp helps the ww to keep in mind the bulb the man with the bulgy eyes turned on and off in the cabin. In that sense it gives the ww what is known as 'direction.'

The city's cemetery, or what's left of it, isn't far away. Up the street (the street called New Street) and over a whip of screaming roadway, Eden is still intact, if hard to get to. It's yonks since the bombs stopped falling.

The ww has been coming to the library for about a week now. Each morning she arrives two or three minutes before opening time, scoffs an apple as she squats, waiting, on the great stone stairs of the entrance, and then, once inside, tosses the core into the bin next to the Issue Desk. The library's rules state that no food is to be brought into the reading room. An apple core doesn't count, though. In the ww's worldview, any substance that has already been masticated no longer counts as sustenance. An apple core isn't food. It's surplus, debris. Let the pips slip through the slim gaps in the wicker bin. Let the core's sugary softness soak into the waste paper (there's never much waste paper in the bins anyroad).

Across the road from the Central Library, which is a redbrick building from the previous century, an ODEON is in the process of being converted into something other than a cinema. It's not possible to tell what, yet. From where the ww is seated, she can see the men removing the enormous O D E O N letters from the side of the building. A man descends the scaffolding carrying the D across him, slung as if it was nothing over his shoulder and balanced on one of his hipbones. The man's workmates cluster beneath him, watching without interest. The ww notices that, so far, the ODEON clockfizzog that sits to the right of the ODEON letters — but now there are only E and O and N, and soon there will only be O and N — the clock has so far been left alone. It's possible that it's too integrated into the building to bother doing much about. And it's useful, the ww thinks. Oversized and easily spotted from the streets around it, the ODEON clock tells the time the way the clocks on churches did once, before everybody wore watches. The ww does have a watch, a thin-strapped one her mom gave to her, but she finds it tricky reading the time from it. The small metal hands are too tiny. To see their clicks the ww has to squint. The ww wears the watch daily, but barely makes use of it.

The ww has recently decided she wants to work on a construction site. The work going on on the ODEON is not construction, but still, it's worth watching. Is that why watches are called watches — because we watch them?

In her hand — she's left-handed and proudly so — the ww grips a see-through plastic biro. Apart from the fact that its body is cracked in places (the cracks reveal the pen's plasticness), it looks like a glass thermometer. The ink is about half way down. It's with this pen or one exactly like it (the ww keeps three biros in her polkadot pencilcase) that the ww is currently at work compiling a set of notes from a copy of *Fowler's Architects, Builders, and Contractors Pocket Book*. The ww is none of the things listed in the book's title. She isn't even a student of architecture.

The book doesn't come from the shelves that surround her. It's borrowed from the ww's dad, who brought it home from his office in Eden when the Corporation gave him retirement. There's no real reason for the ww to be sitting in the Central Library each morning reading it, *Fowler's*, but being here gives her purpose, 'direction.' It helps her to concentrate. Illegally pinned to the low wooden panel above her deskspace is the card given to the ww by the man she met in the cabin, the man who poured her the whiskey. Along with the fizzing bulb, the card is helping the ww to sweat the month out.

The scowling librarian seems not to be around today. In her place is someone younger, a boy the ww vaguely recognises. Hair wilts sleazily across his forrid. Oblivious to the ww's dirty glances, he picks and strums an acoustic guitar covered with stickers. Collapsed into one chair with his feet up on another, the boy is practically horizontal. The glances the ww is giving him are not because of the music *per se*, but because of the music's lullaby sweetness. The ww hates anything folky.

"Hey."

From behind the counter of the Issue Desk, a vaguely familiar fizzog rises heavily up to her.

"Believe it or not, I'm trying to read."

The boy blankly smashes his eyelids. The ww categorically decides not to recognise him.

"!"

"?"

"!"

Back at her section of desk, the ww sucks contemplatively on the end of the biro, watches the man who was carrying the big D scuttle back up the ladder to fetch the E, scribbles something quickly to get the biro's ball rolling, settles down, at last, to work. *Fowler's Architects, Builders, and Contractors Pocket Book* is almost one thousand pages long. It even says so on the inside cover. It's kind of boastful the way the book announces its own fatness, the ww thinks, but still, it's true that one thousand pages is a lot for a pocket book. On the page after the inside cover is an advertisement for a 'Great Paint Organisation.' The advertisement includes an engraving of a bonneted woman poking her nose out the window of a horse-drawn carriage. Turning the page (the ww turns it with great emphasis) she sees a second advertisement. Taking up a whole page of *Fowler's*, this recommends the wares of a manufacturer of 'High Grade Drawing and Surveying Instruments.' The products the manufacturer makes include slide rules, drawing instruments, and office stationery. At this, the ww stiffens. Her freckles cluster in the dips of skin between her cheeks and her nose and also on the strip of skin that goes over her nose.

The city cemetery, what's left of it, isn't far away. Eden is still intact but hard to get to if you are a pedestrian.

At seventeen and one quarter years old, time is already shrinking for the ww. Up until a couple of months ago, the future was all raw possibility. For the ww, at seventeen, the future could have been anything. The future could *be* anything. Also, it wasn't her future that the ww daydreamed about, it was *the* future. A unitary future. A fast, sweaty, steamy future, enormous yet poignant: that was how the ww, who lived comfortably in a house with frilly pillows, who had got rid of her virginity as soon as humanly possible, who swallowed four aspirins daily, two in the morning, two before sleeping, whose only remotely embarrassing habit was collecting the supplements that sometimes came with *The Post* — that was how the ww saw things. The future would arrive and it would be exciting, but it wasn't her responsibility to do anything about it. The way the ww *was*, the way she really thought about everything, the way she read books that none of the other girls at school did — all this would magically transform into the future. That was the way the ww felt about things until a couple months ago. Eden was still intact. There it was, the complex of buildings in which her dad had worked until recently. There was what was left of the bombed-out cemetery by the cathedral: the ww's grandad had died in the cemetery and her school buzz went past its rubble daily. Over there was the open end of the new ring road, the real inner ring road not the quick strip of roadway that now swam around Eden: tubes collapsed out of it; it was making its way around the city, cradling the city or collaring it depending on your perspective. Not that the ww had ever really thought about it until recently. At seventeen years old, the ww didn't think much about road-construction. But then, when the ww was seventeen and one quarter years old, things changed.

First the ww discovered that her mom and dad were not her mom and dad; then she realised, thanks to a schoolfriend who came into class registration one day and announced that she was going to live for a year in Africa, that her school years were about to end. It dawned on the ww that school would no longer be there both to frame the future and simultaneously keep the future at bay, to keep it dangling in front of her. It moreover dawned on the ww that she had no clue whatsoever as to who she was going to be when school finished. Her so-called mom had suggested that if she didn't know what she wanted to do, then why didn't she think about training to be a school Tis'er. At this, the ww had mock-choked on her faggot. Why was that what girls were always expected to do, teach? Why was it — and this is what the ww had eventually come up with in her diary, then come back down with to the kitchen, steadied like a silvery bullet between her front teeth, very shiny — why was it for girls to pass things on impassively? To bear things and get things born? The ww's so-called mom hadn't said anything. The kitchen had smelt tartly of apples. The ww's mom had been making apple crumble.

  The ww doesn't want to bear things. The ww wants to build things, but first she wants to destroy things. Thanks to a really momentous realisation brought on by a really ordinary portable stapler, the ww has adopted the mentality of what is known as a bulldozer. As would anyone who has recently realised that being born and dealing with it is not in the end all that different from being obliterated and dealing with it, the ww wants to destroy things and then to build things. That's why she has sniped this copy of *Fowler's*. That's why the ww *is* going to work on a construction site. The ww is going to work on the new inner ring road, the construction of which involves the destruction of Livery Street, and loads of other stuff, and which makes you wonder what in the world the word 'constructive' means anyroad. Life is a pile of nonsense. The ww wants to work on a construction site. But for now the ww is working quietly in the Central Library.

Through one part-opened window in the reading room, a breeze sneaks. The ww's bobbed hair is too short to be blown by it.

Having turned to *Fowler's* 'Index' and found her page, the ww readies a copy of the *Concise Building Encyclopedia* for additional reference. Behind her, the greasy boy burps softly. At the top of page one hundred and sixty in *Fowler's*, written in capitals, is the word:

CONCRETE

Indenting the paper heavily, the ww underscores this word with her biro, then begins reading the entry printed beneath it. Her mouth makes the shapes of the words as her eyes pass over them.

'Concrete is really a form of artificial stone formed by mixing cement or an hydraulic lime (the cementing material) with some hard material (the aggregate) such as broken brick or stone...'

Tilting her head sideways, the ww carefully writes 'aggregate' and 'broken brick or stone' in her notebook. 'Broken brick or stone': there is (this is what the ww thinks) still plenty of that left around these parts. For some reason this thought makes the ww flush, so, turning around to look at no one (there is no one else in the reading room apart from her and the boy behind the Issue Desk), she checks that no one has noticed.

'... such as broken brick or stone which contains a wide range of particles of all sizes down to sand. The whole is thoroughly mixed with water...'

Across the ww's brain scuds a memory of a Biblical parable about a man who built his house on sand. What happened to the man who built his house on sand? The ww does not quite remember. The only thing she remembers is that the man who built his house on sand was considered foolish despite the fact that, according to *Fowler's*, even buildings built from concrete are sandcastles when it comes down to it. The ww prods at her memory of the parable for more information, but soon her memory has scudded away from her. The mention of water has meanwhile made the ww thirsty. Sucking on the top of the biro helps with this.

'... and sets as a hard, dense homogenous mass. Owing to its superior qualities for the purpose, especially its power to set hard through the body of the concrete, Portland Cement and similar cements have almost entirely replaced lime for this purpose.'

The ww doesn't know what Portland Cement is, so she looks it up in the *Concise Building Encyclopedia*. Entered in the corner of this book's inside cover is the letter 'b', then the numbers 1, and 9. The entry for 'Portland Cement' comes immediately below an entry for 'Portico.' 'Portico' has its own picture: an illustration of a classical porch with four columns, which the text next to the illustration classifies as 'tetrastyle.' The ww allows her eyes to dawdle over the picture for a bit — it looks exactly like the old Town Hall across the road from Eden — then her fingers slip on the page, and paper cascades until the encyclopedia falls open on the entry for — it falls open on the entry for 'Plan.' The ww shrugs, reads:

'The top of view or horizontal section of an object as projected in orthographic projection. Anything drawn or represented on a horizontal plane, as a map of the horizontal section of a building.'

Next to this piece of text happens to be a grainy reproduction of a photograph of a concrete placing plant. The ww meticulously copies out the picture for the hell of it. The plant's diagonal slices and skeletal towers are easy to align, thanks to the gridded background of her notebook. After completing the drawing and feeling pretty satisfied with her draughtsmanship, the ww at last discovers that Portland Cement is

'... a mixture of lime, silica, and alumina, in approximately the proportions of 60, 20 and 10 per cent respectively, with oxides, alkalis, etc. The mixture is formed into a slurry.'

The ww attempts to memorize this. The word 'alumina' dangles around her ears as she repeats it (it dangles like a glittery earring). The word 'slurry', by contrast, sounds dirty. Like 'slutty.' Or like 'slapper.'

Across the road from the Central Library, the ODEON letters are nearly all down now. Only the O and the N remain. Threads of dead neon hang from the N. The O is neatly framed by one of the glass panels of the library windows. This makes the ww think first of a gob gawping open, then about a woman called Olsy. Then before she knows it another of the men is swinging the O over his neck and descending the rungs of the ladder. Below him his workmates steady the ladder's base with bent arms, spread their legs, wolf-whistle at something or someone. The ww nibbles at the biro, corrects a spelling mistake she's made in her notes, returns to *Fowler's* discussion of concrete.

'Concrete made from lime is, however, a material of great antiquity. For example it was used with considerable skill by the Romans.'

The ww notes this in her notebook. The system she uses when taking notes is as so: on the left hand side of the page she writes down either direct quotations or her own paraphrases and also does some sketches, and on the right hand side she adds comments and notes-to-self and doodles that relatively frequently have nothing obviously to do with the topic of construction. Adjacent to *Fowler's* fact about concrete being used by the Romans, the ww writes: PANTHEON / pandemonium / the birth of industry / industrial birth / the brummagem empire.

From behind the ww comes the bump and echo of hollow wood crashing. The boy behind the counter has fallen asleep and dropped his instrument. Up the street and over a screaming whip of roadway, out of Eden and into a sleek motorcar steps the man the ww met in the cabin. The motorcar's numberplate spells out

B3 E B0B.

As he steps into the driver's seat, the man glances briefly up at one of Eden's windows.

The ww sees none of this, and there is nothing in the world that is concrete.

Ten laps of the clockfizzog later, the ww is in the basement of a bar in New Street. Chairs similar to those in the Central Library stand around the room, but in here the seats are sticky and soiled, about to snap if sat at on at the wrong angle. The ww is balanced on one of them. The basement's soupy air has stained the ww's cheeks a deep red colour. Lights cavorting out from a metal rack above the bar's counter paint her cheeks green periodically, then when the lights rewind they go back to red again. The basement is quiet except for the collective slur of twelve or so people, who are mostly, apart from the ww, young men dressed in jeans and t-shirts. For the moment no sound is coming from the two massive speakers that stand next to a raised area in the basement's corner. The lights do their manic dance to no music. The lights dance to nothing.

Up against the ww is of one of the young men dressed in jeans and a t-shirt. The young man's thighs are as skinny as the ww's. His torso, stooped but still tallish, is almost skeletal. The ww has an arm curled around it. The young man's hair is about the same length as the ww's, but much thicker. Compared to the mop of the boy librarian in the Central Library, this mop is freshly washed. It's lustrous in a good way. The young man's name is Terence, but he prefers, as we already know, to be known as Zero.

On the wall behind the ww and Zero are eight faint

letters — K A R D O M A H — but this is not the name of the bar they are in. The faint letters were what remained when the bar's name was swopped for a new one and all the old individual letter signs were taken down by the new owners. They are there because the letters that spelt the old name protected the paint beneath them from years of coffee breath and cigarette dirt, from the bleary burps and bleary sentences of those who once used to congregate in this basement, so many of them themselves ghosts now.

Zero is clean shaven. His eyes are sullen in a poignant way (that's what the ww thinks). He has a few small pimples on his forrid, but nothing explosive. The ww saddles up to him still closer.

"I can't believe we haven't done it yet. When are we going to do it, Zero?"

Zero unclenches a closed fist from a sweating beer can. Laid out flat on the table, his fingers show off a slender elegance. The ww really loves Zero's fingers.

"Do what, bab?"

The ww tenses. One ruby cheek turns green and twitches.

"Don't call me that. You know what I'm talking about."

"Do I?"

His fist wrapped back around the beer can and bringing it up to meet his mouth now, Zero slides his eyes away from the ww. The ww bumps her shoulder against him.

"Come on, Zero."

The ww's heart is dying of impatience. Is it unattractive, her being so forward about things?

"Is it unattractive, me being so forward about things? Is that it? I'm too forward?"

But the most Zero says is:

"..."

The ww continues.

"It's not like you'd be denting my cherry, or whatever."

"Taking. Not *denting*."

"Are you sure?"

He nods.

"OK."

Zero is staring at his beer can as if it was an extraterrestrial. On the raised area by the speakers, a drummer has started soundchecking. Zero closes his eyes, smiles. The ww sneaks a kiss of an earlobe.

Zero changes the subject. So does the ww.

So does Zero.

"Where were yo today, bab?"

"What? Don't call me that."

"Soz."

The ww bursts out laughing, snipes Zero's beer can, tips it, enjoys the metal's sheerness on her lips and the sizzle of the beer on her tonsils. Zero goes to take the can back from her but the ww keeps her grip on it, and, when Zero's fingers retreat, she cranks the can's ring pull off (when it comes off it makes a clicking sound) and then sets the can back down on the table. Under the dazzle of the bouncing lights, Zero gets up, goes to the bar, comes back with two new cans. Fresh sweat-bubbles swim down the sides of them.

"Sweating it out."

Her mouth hardly opened when she said that.

"What?"

"That's what I was doing today: sweating it out."

Zero squeezes the ww's knee tenderly. The ww looks at him, disgusted.

Zero looks at the ww cautiously.

"Where?"

"The Central Library. Opposite the old ODEON. They were taking the letters down. They left the clock, though."

"..."

"Signs stand for nothing, Zero."

The ww nudged Zero in the ribs when she said that. Zero's jeans reach right to his waist, which is non-existent.

"The Romans built buildings with their meanings carved into them. In stone. Did you know the Romans used concrete?"

Zero scrapes his fingers through his hair, mutters:

"I don't know much about concrete."

The ww snorts, grates her chin gently against her can's rim, sips some beer, continues.

"This is what I was thinking about today. Labels, names,

or whatever. Once upon a time, functions were physically part of the buildings, cut into them, built into them. They were unbudgeable. A building was built to be its function. But now we build buildings with temporariness built into them. They can be anything. They swap functions at the wiggle of a finger. But the outlines of the old names hang around. Literally. The ODEON's neon letters have been removed because they could be, but if they'd been carved in stone they wouldn't have bothered. To remove them. They'd have just stuck another sign above them and we would have been expected to know instinctively which sign it was that mattered. They left the ODEON clock, though, even though it's got the ODEON letters on it."

Zero was looking bored before, but when the ww said that last sentence, he perked up a bit.

"They left the clock?"

"Yeah."

"Why?"

"I don't know."

It took Zero five minutes to do his soundcheck. The ww left in the third. Zero noticed her go, but didn't make anything of it. Under a grimacing sky, the ww starts walking homewards. In a moment the sky is falling. The ww doesn't blink: she just continues walking, shudders, gets soaked, gets into bed with wet socks on. Zero's lovely fingers are the second from last thing she thinks of.

It takes the ww the whole weekend plus the first two days of the next week to get over the cold the wetness works up in her. For most of that time she stays bundled in a duvet in her bedroom. Though she does accept the plates of nourishment that her so-called mom brings into her bedroom at intervals, and though there's still so much the ww is baffled about, the ww can't be bothered to be anything but ill at the moment. For four days straight she stays in her room, listening to music through headphones. For four days she does nothing but read, sleep, crunch apples sandwiched between cheese, watch her so-called mom take out the washing in a tub and daub it across the garden, tracing careful detours round the well cavity, where the ww's so-called dad hovers for hours on end, tinkering or just standing there. The ww crouches out of sight whenever the figure hanging the washing rotates and raises two yellowy eyes to the ww's window. The pegged bedsheets pop when the wind blows them. Every so often the ww spies toenails in the slit between her door and the carpet and, occasionally, when she gets up to go to the toilet, she can hear the telephone ringing in the hallway beneath the bathroom. The person on the other end is never Zero. Zero has never called her. Zero never calls anyone.

Eden isn't as close now.

By Tuesday, the ww is delirious. It's enjoyable,

almost. It gets to the point at which the ww is convinced she is hallucinating, which is quite exciting, because the ww has always wanted to try hallucinogens, but hasn't yet had the opportunity. At some point in the morning, she goes down to the pantry and discovers three full tubs of pink paint in a cupboard. Why she goes down to the pantry she doesn't really know, and why there's pink paint stored in there amongst all the piled cake tins and unopened cigar packs, she can't say, either. But the ww nonetheless takes the paint back to her room along with a paintbrush she finds plunged into a tumbler. After removing all the clothes (she spreads them out on the bed very carefully, tracing detours round the two piles of supplements that are still there, standing silently in the middle of her bedroom), she spends two hours painting an image of an elephant on the inside of her wardrobe. The ww inhales the chemical smell of the paint deeply, feels wonderful. Then, after working for half an hour or so, the ww vomits in her knicker drawer. The vomit has the appearance of apple crumble. The ww wonders whether it's more than a cold, this sickness that's come upon her.

Then it is Wednesday, and all of a sudden the ww feels better. The grogginess gone from her forrid and the sludge in her throat evaporated, or mostly, she gets up early, brushes her hair for the first time since Friday, and is out of the house before her so-called parents have turned their bedclothes.

The sun is all over the place at the moment (this is what the ww thinks). Last Friday it was wiped out, weak, rusty.

Today it is fiercely brilliant, a red iron poker stabbing the sky. Or else it's a cigarette burn the same as the one on Zero's forearm. Zero, the ww knows, does that sort of thing to himself for the hell of it. He picks at scabs to improve the proud flesh, which is the phrase he says where the ww would say 'scar.' He snags a suck of someone else's cigarette then instead of taking a drag on the cigarette puts it out on himself, his own flesh. On the skin above his thin long fingers — on the section of arm that's most visible when the hand beneath it is gripping a fretboard — on that bit of skin is an angry circle, within which, when you look closely, are more circles. A scarry whorl, dense, protruding. To think of Zero is either to think of his fag burn or his fingers.

Today the ww would like to be doing gambols in the sunbeams, but she isn't; she's walking in to the Central Library. Either the fever that was in her is gone completely, or its work in her is complete. It could be that the ww is in that bit of an illness where the fever seethes in a way that makes you feel scorching as in on top of the world, not at the end of it, but whatever, the ww is out of her so-called parents' cottage and feels better for it. On her walk into town, which isn't direct but a detour, taking her down the road to Lozells and past her school and then back into town again, all for a reason the ww has no idea of, she sees i) a queue of women with rope-net shopping bags and men with brown leather briefcases wiggling away from a pole-in-the-ground-buzz stop; ii) a gap in a terrace of houses that only a bomb could have made; iii) a row of skinny chickens suspended upside down in a shop window. Beneath the chickens, on a green-turfed table (the turf is plastic), are yams. To the ww's so-called parents, a yam-yam is not a vegetable but someone from west of B19. The ww calls yams sweet potatoes. They taste good; iv) *Simpson's* the fishmonger, 'est. 1790'; v) the cabin in which she had her meeting with the bearded man who poured her the whiskey.

The cabin confuses her at first, because it's not where it was when she was in it. It's moved on. It now sits, squeezed, between two tall redbricks on a road not far from Livery Street. Just down the road from it is no road, but only sandstone and machines and men in hardhats eating sandwiches.

The ww sees a pigeon. The pigeon is dead. It lies prostrate on the ground, a small puddle of blood beside it. The way it's lying makes it look as if someone shot it. The ww feels no sorrow. The pigeon is dead to her. She is dead to the pigeon. The sun will suck its blood up in no time. This is what the ww thinks.

The dead pigeon is only a few yards away from the Central Library. Inside the doors, Zero is already there on the great stone stairs that lead up to the reading room. This stuns the ww, so that all she can say when she sees him is —

"Zero."

— but then, without flinching, she walks straight past him. He strides behind her, grabbing her hand, running up suddenly and hugging her.

"Stop it."

Zero is beaming.

"This is nice."

The ww follows his eyes across the marble handrail and carved wooden banisters, then down to stony floor and frescoed walls. All of this — the banisters, the stone, the frescoes — all of this is condemned, soon to be bulldozed.

Zero repeats himself.

"This is nice."

"I prefer concrete."

Zero steps on ahead of the ww to the top of the stairs, not listening. The ww follows slowly. The stairs are slipping away from her.

"Is everything OK, bab?"

The ww doesn't notice what Zero has just called her. He reaches out a hand and pulls her to him.

"Bab?"

The ww's head is back on her neck again. The dizziness gone as quickly as it came upon her, she goes through the door of the reading room. Zero slots in after her. The scowling librarian and the greasy one are both in the reading room this morning; they look first at Zero and then the ww, then back at Zero, then, with raised eyebrows, back to whatever it is they were busy doing beforehand.

The ww says:

"Racists."

"Hey."

But the ww is already seated, already turning the pages

of *Fowler's*. Zero pulls out the chair next to her. The leather cushion lets off a hushed trump when he sits on it, meaning it must have a rip in it somewhere.

"Where've yo been?"

"Whisper."

"Where've yo been?"

"Quieter."

Zero presses his forrid into the armflesh beneath the ww's shoulder, kisses the flesh, speaks into it.

"I was here yesterday morning. The day before, too."

The ww pushes *Fowler's* aside and contemplates first Zero's fag burn and then his burning irises, which now are turned up to her. The ww pulls *Fowler's* back towards her, but doesn't open it.

"Come to a show on Saturday."

"Another one?"

"Come and then come somewhere with me."

The ww opens *Fowler's*, dogears a corner.

"Where?"

"A place I found."

"What for?"

The ww is teasing him now. Then very quickly she isn't teasing him.

"Zero, I'm adopted."

"What?"

"Want to know who my mom is?"

Zero nods. In the ww's eyes, he's seen something silent

forming.

"Her sister."

"Yower mom is her sister. What?"

" ..."

" ..."

"My mom is my mom's sister. Her name's Olsy."

Zero nods again. The ww had not even realised her mom had a sister. Olsy, her mom's older sister. Olsy, older sister, ol' 'sis, Olsy. When the ww had the momentous discovery that came as a result of her search for the portable stapler with which she intended to staple the supplement that turned out to have as its topic the construction of the inner ring road, the ww went downstairs and asked her mom who Olsy was. Olsy was the ww's mom, her mom had said. When the ww asked what that meant, the bab said that Olsy was her older sister. When the ww had asked, again, who Olsy was — and this was possibly the most confusing thing her mom had said that day — her mom had just said:

"Fabulous."

"Hey, Zero, want to know what asbestos is?"

Nothing.

"Hey. Want to know what asbestos is?"

Zero doesn't answer again, so the ww just tells him.

"An incombustible mineral of a fine fibrous texture. It is used extensively in building, either alone or combined with other materials, where fire-resisting properties are required."

Zero shrugs. He doesn't have anything to say about

asbestos. The ww doesn't, either. Instead she stares at the whorls in his cigarette burn, sniffs snottily.

CONVALESCENCE

B24

A small girl, seated. Seated next to her a man, the girl's dad. The girl in her Worlds End uniform and the dad in a bad pink shell-suit. The girl's nose the same as the dad's except for the fact there's no moustache beneath hers. The girl and the dad raking the flesh of baked potatoes in a cafe, its walls yellow, its air salty, its name miraculously the same as the girl's gran's nickname. The cafe they are sat in is called 'BAB's.'

"What did they teach you about in school today?"

"Not much. Nothing."

A butter slab melting. The cafe's ceiling goose-pimpled.

"They taught you about nothing?"

"*Yes.*"

The cafe's walls yellow. Its windows smeary. The potato flesh smoking.

"Nothing."

"*Yes.*"

"Wow. Nothing. I never learnt about that stuff when I was your age."

The girl's stomach curdling, rumbling. The worry of there not being enough spare butter slabs in the glass bowl next to the toothpicks.

"Hey, close your mouth when you're eating."

In a pot in the middle of the table, tooth picks. In the girl's stomach only cabbage, semi-digested, and the serious worry of there not being enough butter slabs.

"Close your mouth or the wind will change."

The cafe's windows smeary. Beyond them, pavement and fuzzed sunbeams, same as always. Heads spinning. Bare legs, rushing. Cars parked, their bottoms touching. Worlds End in one direction and in the other NEXT, where the girl's mom works. There never being any wind never mind it ever changing. The only rainbows being rainbows made out of concrete, concrete rainbows like the one that hits the ground running near where the girl lives. The girl already knowing that there is not a pot of gold at the end of the rainbow, because the end of the rainbow is where she lives, and she's tried digging. Spit sizzling on the pavement. The baked potato plus butter being the girl's first supper, a secret. The choice of salt or another butter slab being a really big question. The girl's dad swiveling a toothpick contemplatively. His potato flesh impaled on his fork and swallowed before hers has been barely started. His moustache food-flecked. The window smeary. Then the girl's dad suddenly stopping swiveling the toothpick and looking dead on at somebody who's walking through the door and making the cafe's bell squeal.

"Who's that, dad?"

"No one."

But it obviously being someone.

The sadness the girl feels when she realises someone else is sad. The sadness of other people's sadness. The way the girl sometimes looks at her mom or her dad or one of her brothers and there another world is, collapsed across this one in the same way a sheeting of snow collapses across a garden, beautiful and difficult to move through. How sad she feels when snow really falls, as if confirming the existence of metaphorical snow. The girl's mom always insisting that she wear three thick pairs of socks before she goes out into it, the snow.

Understanding what a metaphor is.

"Who *is* it, St. John?"

The girl calling her dad by his first name because her two older brothers, twins, call the girl's mom by the girl's mom's first name. So the girl calling her dad by his first name therefore being the girl's idea of fairness, or at the least, symmetry.

"Honestly, it's no one. It's Zero."

The girl not getting it and not laughing.

"Who's Zero?"

The dad's grin withering.

"Ask your mom."

This being what the dad always says when he already knows the answer. The girl first groaning, then shrugging.

"OK."

"..."

"St. John?"

"Yes. What."

The girl not telling her dad honestly that she doesn't want to go to school anymore and instead telling him that she wants to build a time machine.

"Like *you* said."

"Like I said?"

"*Yes.*"

"..."

The someone called Zero glancing at the girl's dad as if he's felt a feather brush him and he's wondering where it's flit from and then almost as soon as he glances, glancing away again. The someone called Zero evidently saying something extremely funny to the woman stood behind the counter. His hair densely black. There being something about Zero's fingers but the girl not being able to see quite what. The cafe's windows smeary. The girl still barely started on her potato but, at the same time, the girl completely ravenous.

"Like you said when we were in here last week. You said the fall was a thing that had happened once but that was always happening and that *that* was like a time machine combined with a time bomb and that *that* was like a time capsule buried and dug up again each day forever."

The girl not adding that she had also been wondering what would happen if you put the fall inside a time capsule and buried it. That being too mind-boggling. The girl's dad still distracted by the man called Zero. The girl elbowing him, her dad. Him eventually turning towards her. As soon as he does, the girl tucking into her potato.

"The fall? They teach you that stuff too?"

"*Yes.* The vicar said it in assembly, remember."

"The vicar said it in assembly?"

The girl nodding furiously.

"The fall and the garden of Eden."

"The garden of Eden. Don't you know about Eden already?"

"Yes."

"OK."

The potato too hot and so the tip of the girl's tongue getting scolded. Zero leaving with a polystyrene box gripped in a fist without all its fingers.

"Well, how about we settle for a time capsule."

"OK."

"OK, Rita."

In y6, the wind changed.

At Worlds End, the mirrors in the toilets twisted our noses when we looked into them. This was a detail I had never noticed before I became a y6er.

It had always been warm in B24, sunny enough to scram outside whenever it was breaktime; so sunny that, even during winter, the skin on my neck and legs remained forever suntanned. But then in y6 it started raining. The rain broke our breaks, tore stinging tears from their bulbar orbit. I couldn't believe it. The rain that fell was acidic, truly. The bruises it made in the Worlds End ceilings were neon-coloured.

The Tis'ers remained calm. They planned lessons full of varied activities and generally did their best. But y6, those first weeks of it, were difficult. Everything lost its momentum. I lost mine. In y6, a whopping chunk of the world was suddenly lost on me, lost to me. Even breaktimes were eternally broken. For the first time in my life a silence sad and heavy sunk into the silence that had been nothing much but a considered contemplation of what was going to be on TV later. I still wondered what was going to be on TV later, obviously.

On the days that St. John picked me up after school, we went, straight away, to eat baked potatoes in the cafe that was half way between Worlds End and our house. This meal was our first supper. The one prepared by my mom later on in the evening was our second. We never dared tell my mom we had eaten already. The recurring yodels of "NEXT" by the dinner ladies at Worlds End made the Worlds End dinner queue an uncomfortable place to be in, so I never felt like eating much except cabbage at school dinnertimes. I ate all the cabbage and left the scoop of mashed potato unshoveled, which was the opposite of what everybody who sat at my table did. By the end of the day I was starving, and eating two suppers was nothing. Nothing.

The rain came, slapped the windows. Invisibly bitter water dripped into buckets positioned at intervals. It rose invisibly, too, unsteadied my feet, brought on nosebleeds, as if a UFO had landed on the concrete slab that was our playground and everybody had seen it, except that for some reason nobody had the audacity, or certainty, or ability to shout about it.

Whether or not your dad's car had a catalytic converter fitted, this was a big question in y6, one you couldn't get away with not answering. We played spin-the-bottle under the canopies as the rain hissed above us; watched, disgusted, as pairs of gobs worked together frothily. Insults started getting spat around constantly. Indy came in to school one day and presented me with a gold-edged box containing a necklace. The box, it turned out, came from her mom's bedroom. Inside was a faux pearl necklace. Indy's dad's car did not have a catalytic converter fitted, but, as she blurted out to the group that had gathered in the World's End cloakroom, her mom had had a coil fitted: she couldn't make any more brothers and sisters for

Indy even if she wanted to. Indy obviously hadn't needed to add this. She got teased for adding it. She got teased for giving me the the gold-edged box containing her mom's necklace. One of the boys, after first turning pale, stabbed Indy with a lit cigarette butt and then told her to go back to where she came from, which was nonsensical, because Indy came from where we all did.

At Worlds End, by y6, we all knew what a coil stopped. I don't know how we knew.

It wasn't always like this. In spite of the rain and the blistering ceilings, the days remained insanely sunny. We snipped cuttings from newspapers we'd never heard of priced according to units that meant absolutely nothing to us — what did the dinky *d*s mean, we wondered, and how many *s* made up a penny? The snippings were themed according to the project our Tis'ers had set us, a project that was intended to teach us history, maths, geography and religious studies simultaneously, so that we didn't notice what we were learning. We pasted the newspaper cuttings into scrapbooks. Our project was about the building of the road that passed right by the Worlds End playgrounds, the A4400. The A4400 had once been known as the 'inner ring road.' An aborted segment of it swung almost above the Worlds End buildings. The road was begun many years ago and parts of it had since been dismantled. For our project we made maps of its routes (which had changed many times in the course of its planning, and construction, and dilapidation); examined, with Worlds Ends' few microscopes, blades of grass plucked from the roadside. The blades of grass seemed fine to me, very grassy-looking, but they were really, we were told, extremely dirty. Fair enough. We weren't given any other blades to compare them to. Indy showed me how to turn a dirty blade of grass into a trumpet. I was amazed by this, and could never manage to do it as well as she did. There was a room without windows that had a few computers in it and on these we programmed a green turtle to go round and round in a circle without stopping.

Incredibly, we, I, even tolerated the tasks that involved sewing. Up until y6, no Tis'er had ever trusted us with a needle. Though my lazy eye was a disadvantage, I turned out to be fine at threading needles. I was good at steering a needle, ready threaded, through the translucent top sheet of skin on my finger then letting it dangle: once pierced by the thin prick of metal, the skin remained sturdy and never hurt me. I would strut around the classroom, the needle tossing gambols, a deranged puppet or surplus digit. The Tis'er never scolded me. She just told me that if I kept on doing it the piercings would eventually destroy my fingerprint, scar its contours forever. I didn't really see the harm in that.

The rain came down astonishingly thickly. The Worlds End classrooms, which never had been exactly pristine, became ever more swampy, stuffy, hotter, more moldy. The vicar, our vicar, same one as the church I went to, came in to assembly at the head's invitation and told us stories of Biblical cities and how they had fallen. After assembly our Tis'er said we should take his words to heart, but not too seriously. It was her way of teaching us about metaphors, I suppose, but what she said troubled me. I wanted to take the vicar's words very seriously. I wanted to take them literally. I put up my hand to ask what would happen if we did so, if we took what he had said literally, but either the Tis'er didn't see my hand or she ignored me. That particular Tis'er was very thin. When she leant over you to check your workings, or to correct a spelling mistake if you were the kind who made them, her breath smelt faintly of vomit. The Worlds End Tis'ers thought we didn't notice that sort of thing, but of course we did.

There was an A-Z in our classroom containing information about B24, our area. We had to take turns using it. Like pogs and marbles and millions — the sweet pink orbs we washed our cabbage down with, covertly sprinkled on whatever that day's official pudding was — the A-Z became a highly sought and fought over item.

St. John said I should title my scrapbook *The Decline and Fall of the Inner Ring Road*. He said it scanned well and that my Tis'er would get it. I didn't get it. I didn't care much. I think part of the problem was that I already knew what there was to know, in a way. Us y6ers had been absorbing the A4400's dross and flotsam ever since we'd been born, which was ever since all the waters in the world had broken. We breathed its phlegm in daily, played carelessly as it screamed past us, went to and fro on the segments of it still in use, held our breath in the underpasses. The twins — I knew this but didn't know quite how to include it in my scrapbook — the twins lived with their mom in a part of B24 built only a decade or so before the road had been started but then almost immediately lopped off by it, lassoed by one of its tendrils. To get anywhere by foot, the twins either had to cross the road, with all the predicaments and impossibilities that involved, or walk for a while along a path that ran parallel to its cold shoulder and then go under through a subway. The subway had once had shops in it; most were closed now, with the exception of a second-hand bookshop that St. John still liked to go to: metal chains flaked against the shutters. Sometimes, so the twins said, fragments of the road fell away from the main structure. The twins collected these fragments, said I could have one to take in to Worlds End if I wanted. At the time I thought this was extraordinarily generous of them. The twins were sometimes so kind to me that I would decide I wanted to marry one of them.

In y5, sadness was sadness: it could be got over and then forgotten. In y6, I began to put things together, but it was as if, by being put together, things fell apart irrevocably. Then thanks to our vicar I discovered that there was already a name for this feeling, a word that everyone, even if they themselves didn't realise it, kept repeating, drumming into me, a word which I thought I saw written or heard spoken everywhere. Everyone was falling over themselves. Fall off, fall out, fall over, fall into, fall down, fall apart, fell apart, fall together, fall by the wayside, fall to pieces, fall through, fall for, etc, etc. To fall for *something* was to be gullible, to be tricked, deceived somehow, whereas to fall for *someone* was to fall in love with them irrevocably. St. John had fallen out of love with the twin's mom. My mom was always falling over, sometimes in ways we would laugh about for ages, but also because (this is what Rita thought) — because she was trying to say that she felt like she was falling to pieces. The acid rain that fell through the Worlds End asbestos and into our buckets, it fell for me and fell into me.

The Worlds End of y5 was the same Worlds End of y6, except now I had broken eyes to see it with and a bad heart beating inside me as I made my way through its classrooms and corridors.

Here is the world I knew about before *The Decline and Fall of the Inner Ring Road.*

B24 was identikit houses and cul-de-sacs and a mess of structures whose functions were not what they had once been: our workhouse/school, for example, but also the cinema-turned-bingo hall and church which was once a swimming pool. B24 was a psychotic burst of tower blocks and roadways that were only half built. There were lift shafts that thrust out of unroofed buildings. In the wasteland that buffered the cul-de-sacs were great gaping mouths of cylindrical pipes that echoed nothing when you yelled into them but which occasionally vomited a dead ladybird or sweet wrapper. I was afraid of going into the pipes because if you went into them they went nowhere. I didn't know whether the tower blocks were the way they were because they were half built, abandoned mid-construction, or because their demolition had never been fully completed. I didn't spend much time thinking about it. I don't think the question ever occurred to me until St. John posed it that way to me.

First the houses, the buildings we lived in, what all Worlds End y6ers and their families lived in. In colour, design and dimension, the houses on the cul-de-sacs (and on the roads that connected them, but then these too *seemed* like cul-de-sacs) — these houses were all exactly without variation the same as each other. Each could easily have been a clone of the other. This meant it was impossible to 'move house' in our area. You might have heaved yourself and your belongings, but the houses you moved between remained identical. Each stood on reinforced concrete foundations, each had a front lawn if only a slip of one, and each had its number nailed into the front door in the same sans-serif typefizzog; none of the houses had names. They housed nothing but houses, either, since nobody, not one inhabitant, ever, had converted their parlour into a newsagent's or erected a pet shop where once had been their front garden. It's possible people had thought of doing so and had not been permitted to, but I doubt it. For all their curt, flat-roofed abruptness, the houses we lived in had a way of commanding your affection and your fidelity, of converting *you*. Inside, the fireplaces were tie-dye tiled and the kitchens decently appointed. The knobs on the ovens were fluted, same as upturned fairycake cases. Lino covered the floors in dusty tones of green and orange. The slap of slippers was all the more satisfying for the absence of carpets. The kitchens had hatches: I never once entered a house amongst those on the cul-de-sacs around Worlds End that did not have one of these, a slot between the kitchen and the eating space. To me they were always a novelty. How weird is it to have your supper passed to you, confirmed as your supper, blessed by the absence of mortar, through a gap in an indestructible wall? That was what Rita thought.

'*Move*, Rita.'

I liked to pass my hand back and forth through the hatch as I watched my mom prepare food in the kitchen. I think I expected the hand to become a hoof, or something.

Second, the reassigned structures. Our church, as mentioned, was housed in a converted swimming pool. We were quakers without a capital Q and diluted Catholics, simultaneously. Everybody was in B24, or at least that was our church's implicit suggestion. Creeds of all sorts crawled the cracked pavements and pebble-dash walls, but our church didn't think of itself as leading one religion amongst, or against, others. It didn't think of itself as having any equivalent whatsoever. In a way that concealed its sly intolerance, our church was totally tolerant: patronising, paternalisitic, though that is not how I, influenced by my mom's total commitment, then thought of it. They didn't even mind sinners in our church, situated as it was on all midpoints, skewered on all fences. You could be divorced, as St. John had been before he met my mom and they made me, and still take a dip in the (now metaphorical) swimming pool; a plunge too, if you felt like it. All were given the same pat on the scalp, which is what I, as yet unconfirmed, got every Sunday as a blessing. All were welcomed. The suggestion was that everyone believed the same anyroad, which was our church's way of saying that, at heart, when you grind it all down, *you* all believe what *we* do. We were the ones that taught you how to believe. We are the ones that will teach you how not to.

For our church was a soggy, soppy church. We went, every week, to the arena that was situated between a curl of houses and the A4400, adjacent to the wasteland. Just as long as you spoke the words correctly, we were counseled, you could interpret them any which way you liked. The words were no longer there to interpret *you*. The services were led by a vicar, same as the one who came in to the Worlds End assemblies. He gave lectures projected from the diving board above what had once been the deep end. The entrance to the arena, an oblong of concrete with vast windows that turned all sunbeams into sparkles, was approached via a sloping track that rose up from the car park. The ramp's purpose, I reckoned, the reason why the building's post-swimming pool inhabitants had kept it along with the emptied pool, was to prepare those ascending it for the worship ahead of them. In the foyer you signed yourself in at the semi-circular desk, or a parent did so for you if you were not yet a y6er, and then you pushed a coin into one of the vending machines. These contained stacked racks of silver loops, spiraled wires, and vended pamphlets containing the day's service and an abridged version of our Holy Book. In a previous life the machines had vended snacks: the booklets that collapsed to the rectangular mouth at the machine's bottom had a vinagery whiff about them. They smelt like raw onions. I once saw my mom licking the spine of one of them. Her eyes were so tightly closed they looked like they'd been glued together, like mine when I blew out the candles on a birthday cake and made some wish or other, which would always be something boring such as 'I wish my mom would love me.'

The ridge of her tongue (my mom's) was spotted with the red lipstick she'd been wearing earlier.

"I don't think you should wear that to church."

"Don't do that."

"It's OK, Rita."

St. John's voice was softer than that of most dads I heard. He never shouted, though his eyes, when he was angry, roared. From that day onwards I took every opportunity I could to lick the books that fell from the vending machines. It was better than letting the smell of chlorine get to you. For some reason, even though the pool was not a pool now but a pit, tiled but dry, the attendants still squirted a spray of diluted chlorine, or what I presumed to be chlorine, before every service. It was intolerable. Even worse were the changing rooms. Their fluorescent signs hissed at you as you approached them, and after that it seemed impossible not to obey their instruction to separate according to gender and enter the respective chambers, even though, once entered, you went no further than removing your shoes and pegging your coat up. If there were other things I accepted about church, even took extremely seriously, I could see no point in this part of it. I hated what I understood to be the room's *memory*, which is to say I hated the thought of all the unswaddled bodies washing themselves off in grotty showers, of bosoms wobbling and cold buttocks puckering. I hated the inherited segregation, too. Hated it. I hated the sickly glow the fluorescent changing room sign smeared on my forehead. I wanted to wash it off me as quickly as possible. But how do you wash off something that isn't really on you anyroad — how do you wash off the ridiculous smear of a fluorescent light?

This was the world I knew before *The Decline and Fall of the Inner Ring Road*.

Third, the unfinished constructions and those that had been abandoned mid-way through their destruction, or those that were by then in some middle state of degeneration. These were many. Like awkward fragments between whole numbers, those digits it was more difficult to do sums with, they even entered in between the repeats of our houses. They existed in miniature as well as in magnitude, in disconnected wiring as well as in the tall uncapped constructions, where machinery stood immobile as it had stood for decades, where the rain that came in y6 collected in buttery puddles, where the horizon was barbed. At dawn, when the sky bled, the cranes bent over these buildings seemed bent in prayer.

The fragments sprawled everywhere. They were there on the edges of our concentration of cul-de-sacs, scattered across the wasteland, there in gardens and weedy allotments. They were for the most part totally normal — odd at times if you stared long enough, or if you discovered a new one, but always easily assimilated back into landscape with which we were comfortable. There was one structure that was different, but it was only different because I, during the project on the A4400, decided it should be, and by deciding so retroactively afforded it importance. I selected it as a special feature of my scrapbook. It was the aborted segment of roadway that swung almost directly above the Worlds End playground. Apparently it had been begun as an overpass, but as it was it halted mid-passage and then stopped, the steel rebars tickling the air where the concrete they were meant to strengthen had dropped away, or possibly never existed. It was a giant's gangplank or elephant's trunk, or else a vertiginous diving board. In the story I wrote about it in y6, I christened this edifice

THE OBSOLISK.

St. John, who was my father, said the choice of moniker was ingenious.

Worlds End was well placed to view it. The Obsolisk overhung the school almost directly, so that, when we were still taking them outside, we were able to calculate our breaks by the shadow it cut across our playground. Time, a thing otherwise described, to my hot and sweaty y6 mind, by Ds and Es and Os and Ns and the spaces between them, could also be worked out according to The Obsolisk's shadow. The patterns cast by its stump, or the stump that The Obsolisk *was*, interacted in strange and incredible ways with the markings already there on the playground, where grids and arcs tangled with astroids and crescents, bullet-noses and tomahawks, all of which could mean anything from a game of netball to a safe haven from the bulldogs to a precarious stepping stone to a prairie. This was already a webbed and irregular world, one chockablock with potential other worlds. And when The Obsolisk cast down its shadow, the worlds multiplied wildly. We would skid in and out between in-shadow crescent and out-shadow crescent. We teetered along the tangent formed by the shadow's kissing of the tomahawks' curve as if it was the brim of a whaling ship and we were courageous harpooners. I say 'we.' I played many of these games on my own, or with only Indy.

Even before y6, even in y5 or y3, I'd seen runs suddenly stutter and the stunned runner come to a stop as abrupt as The Obsolisk's, then bend their head back and gaze up through the glare that, even when the rain came, was always there. I saw this happen to Indy one day towards the end of y5, when the weather was exceptionally hot and the turfed ground around the playground had gone sandy, despite our Tis'ers warnings to us not to ruin it by running on it.

Indy had the kind of eyes that glinted in the sun as

if they were glasses. She never wore glasses. When we weren't playing together, which most of the time meant we were playing on our own, I sometimes watched her from a concrete tunnel that must once have been part of a sewer, but which someone had had cleaned up, sanitized, reassigned to a playground amusement. Indy stood dead still in the middle of the playground. I lay in the hard roll of the tunnel, sculpted to its curve with my feet above me, blood flooding my brain, watching Indy with upside down eyeballs. Eventually, I shuffled out of the tunnel and approached her.

"Indy."

"..."

"Indy. Indy."

"INDY."

"..."

"INNNNDDDDY."

"Yeah, Reet?"

"What are you staring at?"

She turned to me. The glint had tumbled out of her eyes and onto her cheeks. At first I was incensed that she was crying, and then I was devastated.

"Indy, you're crying."

For some reason I felt the need to point this sad fact out to her.

"Am not."

She threw her hands up, covered her fizzog. I tried to pull her hands away again.

"Yes, you *are*. Look, you're crying."

At that point she had stuck out her chin and started rubbing it ferociously. For her this was the worst form of offense it was possible to muster. It was the closest she ever came to swearing. It wasn't exactly appropriate in this context — at Worlds End you rubbed your chin like that when you knew someone was massively fibbing — but I understood. Sort of.

Back inside the segment of tunnel it was cool and dense with small dull echoes. I re-arranged myself. Keeping my legs and trunk contained, I stuck my head out of one end so that my skull rested comfortably. Because of the dislocated hip I'd been born with, I'd had to wear a splint for a while, and because of this I'd slept on my back a lot as a babba, and because of that there was a flat ridge on my crown that was good for carrying books on. I rested the ridge on the ground. A tuft of grass petted my earholes. I shut my eyes, clicked them back open. In the near distance I could hear the constant fizz of the roadway, which was so common to me it was almost nothing. Above was the jilting overpass, carless and silent, yet to be christened The Obsolisk. Raw steel poles, some of them bent back on themselves, poked out of it. Thick columns supported it. Turf bearded it: a membrane of moss, weeds, and flowers, same as the pink ones that spotted the wasteland.

All sorts of possibilities presented themselves to me: that Indy and me would build a den up there; that the broken roadway above me was the portal to another universe and that you just had to step to the edge, believe, and keep on walking and you wouldn't fall but instead walk somewhere you couldn't see except by trusting and walking (this might well have been an adaption of a scene from one of the Indiana Jones movies, after whom, obviously, I assumed Indy had been named); that possibly it wasn't another place the ledge sent you to but another timezone (this was perhaps the beginning of my interest in time machines); that it was a ruin from a fallen city (on this front, I wasn't entirely inaccurate); that it was where God lived (which would have explained why the diving boards had survived the refit in our church building).

The twins never came with us to church. They had their own church, where they went with their mom. I had never, ever met their mom. As they didn't always live with us, I couldn't see why I couldn't marry one of them one day. St. John could explain the obvious: that they were my brothers, that I shared blood with them, and therefore I couldn't marry them. But he couldn't tell me why them not living with us made no difference to this situation. I didn't like to ask my mom these kinds of questions.

In our church, the congregation sat in the shallow end. Where once swam scabs, plasters, and hairbands with hair still clotted around them, there we gathered. The deep end was where the vicar stood. It was also there that the diving board reached out above the tiles, which were white striped with navy. Usually the vicar would wait until each one of the congregation had climbed the seven steps down into the shallow end and found a place to stand, and to sit. He would emerge, capped and goggled in my drawings, fat and dog-collared in reality, and begin the service. Whenever I prayed everything got messy, because I tried to pray about everything simultaneously. From under my knitted palms I would sneak a peak at my mom. For inspiration. Out of curiosity. But my mom would never tell me what it was she prayed for.

~

'Because of the number of old cellars on the line of the road, a considerable quantity of filling has been needed. The material used has been obtained from the demolition work in progress in the city on the clearance of old property in the redevelopment areas. This demolition material consists of brick and hardcore, with a small proportion of mortar and plaster. [...] [W]hen spread in 9 inch layers by means of a D.8 bulldozer and followed by rolling with a 10-12-ton smooth-wheeled roller, [this filling] crushes and compacts to form a very stable base.'

Paper No. 6489, 'The Inner Ring Road'

~

PRECIPITATION

BI, BII, B3, B2

Flapping about in the breeze now chasing the bab away from Eden towards the cemetery are the first, second, penultimate and final pages of *The Post*. On the second page is this headline:

ELEPHANT SKULL DISCOVERED IN LIVERY STREET.

The big text seen by the bab as she trots past the gutter *The Post* has paused in; but the story-text too small to read without stopping. The gutter water bubbly. *The Post* pages soaking. The bab carrying quickly on past banks shutting and sooty shoulders revolving and a surprising percentage of scalps without hats on. The bab dodging the paunch of a man who's walking as if he doesn't have a paunch. Her thinking that the man would no doubt categorically deny he has one even though he can't have had a good view of his goolies for ages. Her trying not to think about what it would be like to have flab like that rumble upon you. Why men's bellies are considered a non-factor in their attractiveness. No-man's land. The air brown and clogged now. The breeze itself cloggy. Another broken building, its roof smashed. Bomb bored. The bab bored of the bombs now. A pigeon impaled on the buttonless pins of a cash register. A fist found clutching a spam tin. An interred perambulator. A wolfwhistle. The bab carrying on past it all up a slight incline towards the cemetery and without properly stopping popping a coin into the barnacled palm of a warbling *Post* seller and then stuffing the rolled-up paper in her handbag. The Grand dribbling above her. The bab crossing and taking her place in the coiling line by the tram stop and after wondering whether it's worth her taking the paper out before the tram comes taking *The Post* out and turning over the first page which is all bombfall as usual, and then reading:

ELEPHANT SKULL DISCOVERED IN LIVERY STREET

Early yesterday morning an unnamed member of the public reported an extremely large and unusual-looking object apparently abandoned in the middle of Livery Street. According to the witness, who was adamant that he had not been intoxicated at the time of his observation, the object approximated the skull of a bulky mammal. It appeared to be sporting two tusks. The witness, who did not give his profession, had at first approached the object thinking it to be a milkcart or apple barrow in difficulty (the witness reported that his eyesight was no longer what it used to be). Being positioned between two tram rails, the witness rightly commented that the object was rather dangerously situated. The unidentified observer gave the time of the incident as being 3.50 AM.[1] He pointed out that had a tram been in operation at that hour, a terrible accident would have been possible.

The witness apologised that he was not able to supply further evidence either in support or explanation of this strange sighting. Having been understandably shocked by his discovery that the strange object standing in the middle of Livery Street was neither milkcart nor apple barrow but instead something 'rather more biological and/or zoological', the witness, who by his own description 'happen[s] to be a founding member of our city's renowned Film Society', rushed into the Society's nearby premises with the idea of extracting

---

[1] In fact, Doug initially informed the *Post* chap who took down his story that he could not in any way be sure at what time the sighting occurred. Doug doesn't wear a watch, and, as Doug pointed out to the Post chap, the cathedral bells can no longer be relied upon. The cathedral bells no longer chime hourly because, like lamplight at night-time, they have been silenced. The reason for this being that if they were to chime on the hour hourly they might attract bombfall. So the only way Doug was able to approximate the time of his sighting as being 3.50 AM was by deduction. Not long before he was walking along Livery Street, Doug had passed by the ODEON at the bottom of New Street and on the ODEON clockfizzog Doug had noted that the big hand was pointing to one of the Os and that the little hand was half way between a / and the N. This meant it was twenty to four. And as after passing the ODEON Doug had turned up Needless Alley, crossed the cemetery, greeted a man having a smoke on the steps of the Grand, and then strolled on down Livery Street — and as this was a route Doug took regularly and knew how long it usually took him — because of all this Doug had reckoned up that he spotted the elephant skull at approximately 3.50 AM.

a reel and movie camera and capturing the strange object on celluloid. Alas, by the time the equipment had been readied and the witness had returned to the spot where he had first made his observation, the object in question had gone. The witness opined that it was probable a dutiful policeman had come across the object in the witness' absence and, realising the dangers of its situation, duly moved it on. As to how the object came to be located in Livery Street in the first place, and as to whether or not it really was an elephant skull — these details for the time being remain clouded in mystery.

REDEVELOPMENT

B2

As it happens, one of the paragraphs the ww copies out of *Fowler's* in its entirety concerns the 'life' of buildings:

'*The annual rate of building has, apart from new developments and expansion of all kinds, a close relation to the need for renewal and replacement of old and outworn buildings. The "life" to be given to buildings is a difficult topic to discuss in a small space. It may, however, be said that there is a widespread desire to see the average actual "life" of dwellings reduced, in order that both in planning and equipment they may be kept reasonably in step with new ideas and a rising standard of living. Some movement in this direction will no doubt be experienced, but it is important to realise that **obsolescence** is not, as some seem to think, mainly a design and technical problem.*'

Later, after she lost first Zero and then Zero's babba, which no one had even known she was carrying, because she stayed practically bellyless for most of the pregnancy, after all-this-and-more-besides, 'life' would become an extremely important word for the ww, though no longer in the context of buildings.

CONVALESCENCE

B24

A quick word about my timekeeping. For my seventh birthday I received two separate presents from my parents. From St. John I unwrapped an umbrella. This came, as St. John's presents always came, out of nowhere. I had not asked for an umbrella and my birthday was in the Spring. The present from my mom was, by contrast, an object I'd asked for. It was an alarm clock. But the one my mom gave me wasn't the clock I'd wanted, the one I'd strenuously circled, with red biro, in the catalogue. It was a themed alarm clock, which is what I had wanted, but the theme she had chosen was wrong. Totally wrong. How she had managed to make such a terrible mistake was beyond me. I gasped loudly when I tore open the wrapping paper. It was OK that I gasped like that because, as a deflating balloon has a way of sounding sad and happy simultaneously, the gasp seemed to succeed in giving my mom the impression that I was delighted. She smiled broadly; I beamed back at her. But what to me was most unfathomable about the alarm clock she had got me was that although it was a themed alarm clock and obviously a child's clock, it was old. Its theme was completely outdated. The clock might have been classifiable as an antique, even. It had dust on it. I was horrified. Instead of the theme I'd wanted, I'd got an 'oscarfizzog', an ODEON alarm clock. This was a clock that told the time according to the ODEON letters, known as an oscarfizzog because ODEON stood for Oscar Deutsch Entertains Our Nation. Clocks of this kind had been popular yonks ago, with children who by now were adults. The only reason I even knew this was because I had once asked St. John a question about the clockfizzog on the facade of the bingo building.

PRECIPITATION

B3

Doug walks home. Doug walks everywhere. To take a tram in the manner of the bab would leave too little space for stick-gesticulating, and Doug, who has walked with a stick ever since his wedding night, is a materialist to the extent that he really does think with his stick. If he's thinking about dinner, then the stick's slice and glimmer has the rhythm of a stomach working over its digestion. The slices bear no relation to a knife preparing an onion. Doug has never once wet his eyes over an onion. He has had one lobbed at him by the hunched and furry grocer who keeps shop on Needless Alley, a man from whom Doug has 'borrowed' many onions. The majority of those onions have been lovely, pert enough for their outer stratum to crunch pleasantly when Doug has squeezed them, though some, admittedly the ones the grocer has chosen to lob at Doug, have been regrettably mushy in places. But onions there must be. They lighten the blood and firm the muscles. Doug's wife, Lotte, uses them a great deal in her cooking. Lotte herself is neither sour nor particularly tangy. It's just that her anal emissions are so high-pitched that Doug mistakes them for onions frying. His stick looses its stickiness when he thinks of Lotte at the chopping board. Her elbows are so *pointy*.

Kicking a non-existent stone and not hitting the lamp-post, then kicking it again and this time closely missing the dainty stele of the Margaretta, Doug makes his staccato way across the city's central cemetery. The sun, as ever, is lacking in enthusiasm. Doug's not massively bothered. The fug and chug of this place has become his fug and chug. The air's noxious ooze he has come to find soothing. Doug, after all, is a big fan of all things intoxicating, and he has found this city's combination of fumes to offer him the opportunity to become intoxicated in a fashion very invigorating. Compared to the country (coincidentally, a location also known by many city people as 'the sticks'), the choice of toxins here is enormous. Doug would have stopped off at the Kardomah Café had he not had to collect the shopping from that hooligan in Needless Alley. Besides producing encouraging gurgles whenever he enters 140 Armoury Road's scullery, collecting the shopping is Doug's only domestic duty. He performs it dutifully. He does not at all find his 'character' compromised by carrying bags of vegetables across a cemetery.

Doug's stick spins through one full circle. It lands with a pang on the gravel, however, when he thinks of the Kardomah.

It's possible that the Kardomah Café could have been Doug's, his very own avant-garde establishment, had it not been for Lotte's objections to the idea of them taking it over from its previous owner. Doug still wonders what would have become of them (by which he really just means himself, Doug) if they had done. That dream was not to be, though. The fantasy was not destined to happen. Instead, Doug and Lotte, when they first moved here, came by a house near a fakteroi and, immediately seeing their opportunity, turned that house into a boarding house. 140 Armoury Road.

Thankfully, Doug does not suffer from agoraphobia, because apart from him the cemetery's trapezoid is at the present moment emptied of all living inhabitants. The pigeons don't count as living. God no. The only creature Doug has ever killed was a body-popping pigeon — he did the deed, as you can imagine, with his stick — but Doug has never considered that incident to count as a killing, because pigeons to him are deadness incarnate anyroad. They rot as they gobble. They are an infestation (Doug's stick, as he thinks this, careers through the air with impressive velocity). Give him frogs and locusts over the fat dirty birds any day. It's a sign of the times, Doug thinks (confusing, as usual, the tangents his thoughts take for the general direction of reality) that plagues should these days be made of pigeons.

In addition to pigeons, Doug's stick has an occasional tendency to abuse his right kneecap. It's possible that it is testing Doug's patellar reflex. It's possible that the motion is involuntary. To the bafflement of the bab, who once noticed the purpling patches around Doug's knee when she and her dad once shared a sunbathing session in the garden of Armoury Road, Doug blames the bruises on the fact that he no longer believes in God nor any notion of the Holy Spirit.

Take that, Bishop Gory! But it's Doug who wobbles.

Doug is always wobbling. Or is it in fact the world, the oversized onion that is Earth? The Earth chucked through the multiverse by a merchant on Needless Alley? Such are the mental movements Doug's stick has the privilege of conducting.

The bab's dad today dons i) round-rimmed glasses with tortoise-shell frames and bleary lenses; ii) a 'crush hat', which is nothing more exciting than a 'top hat' that collapses, allowing those seated behind you the better to feast their eyes on the opera, or, in Doug's case, the screen of a cinema.

The Grand Hotel's windowframes, observes Doug, once he recovers from the exertion of stickily biffing the Bishop Charles Gore in the gob, are currently all glassless. The Grand's window frames are windowless. Into one of the vacant boxes walks a woman. She shakes a dusting rag, then disappears. The dust cloud that outlasts her spreads itself thickly, too thickly for dust. Ascending up above the chimney pots of the Grand, the dust cloud erupts into a flock of birds that are not pigeons. Though charmed by the beauty of this odd instance, Doug doesn't think too much of it. The pop-up thought of porkchops — which itself comes punctuated by a stick-jut to Doug's approximate five o'clock (or as an Oscar Deutsch clockfizzog would put it: big hand on the H, little hand on the O) — meanwhile means that Doug has forgotten to go to the butcher's.

Doug has forgotten to go to the butcher's.

Lotte will be saddened and disappointed, and Lotte's

sadness is capable of casting a bigger cloud over Doug than any dusting rag could ever muster. Doug loves Lotte but Lotte's sadness has a strange way of disgusting Doug. Disgust towards a loved one is a more common sentiment than is often mentioned but is nevertheless not a sentiment that Doug is great at coping with. Doug feels the world intensely. He drinks whiskey to feel it even more intensely but also to feel less of it (the world).

It's not that Doug is an unwilling pork-chop-shopper. On the contrary, Doug usually enjoys visiting the butchers very much. He finds all the rawness refreshing. He has no objection to the severed heads, the trotters, the slippery inners which remind him of on his own, even though he has never seen them (his own inners). He has a ton of respect for the honesty of the blood on the butcher's tabard. To Doug, the butcher's shop signifies an approval of life's embroilment. It never troubled Doug to have intercourse with Lotte during her monthlies, and not for the reason that it reminded him of their wedding night. Nothing broke on he and Lotte's wedding night but Doug's back, and that only metaphorically. In fact, a visit to the butcher's is something Doug finds erotic: entering the shop in all its pinkness is like entering Lotte in all of hers. It's not the sausages that draw his attention, but the blush of the thigh slabs. Doug doesn't mind going to the butcher's. He much prefers going to the butcher's to purchasing onions.

It's just that the visit this time simply escaped him. Situated as Doug's butcher's of choice is to the rear of the

ODEON and not at a convenient point between the ODEON and 140 Armoury Road, the visit this time completely escaped him. Lots of things escape Doug these days, such as: bellyfluff floating around in his bathtub when he tries to pinch it with his fingers; the fact that there are bombs falling; the scissors; his children; his temperance if not his temper (since Doug is perfectly gentlemanly even when a whole whiskey aristotle has been emptied); his stick itself, increasingly.

Given the meal that Lotte is already undoubtedly in the midst of preparing, Doug's meatlessness is an issue that needs to be urgently cerebrated. Doug finds it preferable that all cerebration is done while he is comfortably sedentary. The same goes for most forms of celebration. Think about it: whiskey is simply not a drink to be drunk standing.

Having retreated slightly backwards into the bowels of the cemetery and lowered his buttocks onto the same diminutive grave that his daughter once took a gigantic piss upon, Doug considers his current meatlessness. Because Doug 'is Doug', he combines this attempt to work through his lack of marrow with a recapitulation (stick tap-tapping at the midget's

Memory

), of his progress from gentleman farmer to inner city boarding house landlord. From a facade with eight sash windows so easy to fling wide open — look at the fields! look at the pansies!

— to a facade with

/ / / / / / / /

(Watt's stick counts the apertures of 140 Armoury Road) eight
sash windows best kept closed. From that to this. From this
to that. From mud and stench and onions to soot and stench
and onions. From paying toothless women barely anything to
pick potatoes to paying a hairy grocer nothing at all for a sack
of potatoes. From farting cows to belching chimneys. From
gazing into the skeleton of the house you were born in and
which in a tipsy fever you set fire to and deconstructed to a
skeleton (this is what Doug once did after accidentally spilling
whiskey in the attic of the familial farmhouse; the flames that
then flamed seemed to Doug to be the very same flames Doug
had been chasing ever since he had taken his first sip of whiskey
as a fifteen year-old) to gazing at the rust of the iron railings
that enclose a cemetery, which when it rubs off and sticks to
your fingers turns out to look like dried blood. It would make,
Doug's stick seems to imply as it hops upwards and wags with
an exuberance that is quite magical, a wonderful movie.

The movies happen to be one of Doug's prime topics of
thought. He has seen all movies, pretty much. To have seen all
movies, ever, is not an impossibility at this point (B3) in time
(late afternoon), particularly if your own life outspans that of
the filmic medium, as Doug's does. How many movies had
been made by the time Doug was ten? How many movies had

been made, and let's add to that *seen*, since they would have had to be seeable in some sort of public arena for Doug to have been able to see them, by the time Doug turned a vigorous if hollow-cheeked fifteen? Obviously by the time he grew to twenty, or thirty-three, or forty, or sixty-five, the world's collective collection of celluloid had become more voluminous and things therefore more complicated, but it's still a possibility that, at this exact point (the pint-sized gravestone of Margaretta) in time (big hand N, little hand E), Doug could potentially have seen all movies so far in existence. In other words, the total time 'in' all movies combined could either be $<$ or $=$ to the total time that has 'taken place' in Doug's life. In other words, it's a possibility that the expanse of time bracketed by Doug's first body and his last one, as in the most recent sack of cells to hold together his interior quagginess[1], could either comfortably swallow or perfectly model the amount of time contained in all movies so far ever made, which in itself is equal to the amount of time so far sucked up into a camera. Not that it's necessarily the case that he really could have seen all movies ever. For a start, Doug's film-bufferry only really got going when he arrived here in this city: there were no cinemas out in the sticks when Doug was a youngster. It's probably totally improbable that he has seen all movies ever.

It's also a nice diversion from the glitch of his

---

[1] 'Quagginess' strictly speaking refers to a 'defect in timber consisting of shakes at the centre.'

meatlessness, the lack of porkchops problem.

Oh dear, what a div I am, Jesus, thinks Doug, dancing a provocative stick-glance at the Bishop's statue as he does so. Doug, who despite his distaste for gods and bishops is not at all irreligious, dangles his eyeballs, too, in the Bishop's direction. Doug's gaze is glittery but discernibly sheepish. The Bishop stares back in the only way he can do, which is stonily, but Doug, whose attentiveness is famously irregular, a 'characteristic' complained about by both Olsy and Frank but never, strangely, by the bab or Lotte, is no longer paying any attention to Charlie Gore whatsoever.

Instead, Doug's stick has all but frozen at the thought of trying to calculate not the total time that actually tocks in all movies ever, i.e. the total duration of all movies ever, but instead the total *implied* time, i.e. all the time that is not itself necessarily visualized ('shot') *but* which *has to have passed* in order to make any film's narrative plausible. The time in-between us seeing the hero as a moody young man and us seeing the hero as a broody old man, for example. The time that has *elapsed*, but out of sight, out of picture. Time that has not been captured, but which is both a consequence (an extrusion or exudation) and a cause (a prime mover) of time that *has* been captured. It's a conundrum and a big one. If Doug were to solve it he would be a genius. Doug, though, is no genius. He knows that. He has no pretenses, or at least not many. He is terribly forgetful. He knows all too well that he is at once indefensible and defenseless, which is perhaps why the bab and Lotte go on fussing over him, still. Or perhaps that's merely a cliche. He has no time at all for the pseudo-quackeries of theology or of the psychological sciences, though he does find it curious that his youngest daughter has discovered her vocation drafting a map in Eden. Doug has taken to calling the bab either 'Athanasius'[2] or 'Blavatsky'[3], but neither nickname has stuck, since nobody except Doug knows what on earth Doug is talking about. That is one of his lifelong afflictions.

The stump of stone he sits on has inched its coldness deep into his pelvic girdle.

A figure carrying what seems to be a severed toilet bowl passes nonchalantly across the gravel path. The figure is wearing blue overalls. Inexplicably, but with the speed and decision of a compass arrow, Doug's stick swings in the direction of the Kardomah.

Doug's stick swoops severely whenever he thinks about the Kardomah. This is because whenever he thinks about the Kardomah he inevitably thinks about what it could have been had he, Doug, become its helmsman. Because had Doug been the Kardomah's helmsman, the Kardomah would not merely have been the habitual venue for the chattering practitioners

---

[2]   Athanasius Kircher, cartographer of *Mundus Subterraneus* (c.a. 1665), or 'The Underground World', a text that contains a map of the fabled lost island of Atlantis.

[3]   Helena Petrovna Blavatsky, otherwise known as 'Madame Blavatsky', theosophist and defender of the thesis that the inhabitants of Atlantis destroyed themselves with an overdose of their own supernatural prowess.

of anatopisms — the basement being the favoured haunt of the local group of surrealists — but also the centre of a brumalia of filmmakers. Of movie-shakers. Of cameramen and editors. The coffee shop of choice for a generation of revolutionary directors. That would have been Doug's Kardomah. The atmosphere in there would have been quite literally E L E C T R I C, as the cinema on Station Street, which would be one of Doug's favourites venues were he not by necessity already an ODEON devotee, would put it. The Kardomah under Doug would not be merely have been chock-a-block with artists, whom Doug tends to like so long as they have an interest in the movies. He once posed nude for a painter who ended up using only Doug's fist in the final picture, which left Doug unsure whether to be flattered or insulted.

Oh, thinks Doug, his stick sibilating as he whisks the air with it, it would be so lovely to be landlord of the Kardomah, which would serve Turkish coffee *only* were Doug to have his way with it, for no particular reason other than the fact that Doug enjoys its bitterness. But Lotte was never going to have it. Too much temptation. Too conspicuous. After the incident with the farmhouse, Lotte understandably wanted some peace for her and her babbas. The city was easier to slip to one side in, but not if you were the landlord of the Kardomah. No doubt Doug's grand intentions would anyroad have been scuppered by the fact that this city, despite the rapidly expanding Deutsch empire, as well as the Paramount, the E L E C T R I C, and the Film Society, of which Doug is, to his pride, a founding member

— despite all the city's movie-going and all its industry, this city has never yet been able to weld those two dimensions of itself together. It manufactures celluloid, yes, but decent films, nope. Apart from Doug's own amateur endeavours, this is a city without a film industry to speak of.

The gravestone of Margaretta, still the seat of Doug's cerebrations, shifts in the ground ever so slightly. The fault is not enough to worry Doug, though. He barely lifts an eyebrow.

Cerebrations, celebrations. In a cemetery, what's the difference.

Doug sighs.

Doug swallows.

Doug's stick absently fiddles with the non-existent stone he was kicking earlier. So far, apart from the Bishop, the figure with the severed toiletbowl and the emptied, melancholic window frames of the Grand, Doug has not noticed much about his surroundings. Who does? In novels everybody is always very observant. This is a good thing, on the whole. In novels, the world fizzes, becomes brilliant. Everything that should be felt *is* felt. Everything that shouldn't be felt *is* felt, and everything that shouldn't be felt but *is* felt, is felt. The being of people babbles busily, but so, more crucially, does what is known as 'nonbeing.' This augmented state of awareness on the part of certain characters, obviously not all of them or all of the time, also allows the novel's reader to think to themselves, 'Oh, *I've* spotted that particular thing about that particular thing too', when really, to be honest, they probably haven't.

There are certain dubious types who believe books percolate empathy and intelligence in the same way a place like the Kardomah percolates artistic energy, and that suffocating a shelf with them (books) is enough to help you build up your 'emotional intelligence.'

That said, the question of empathy is not at all equivalent to that of perception. Better watch out for *that* landmine, Doug thinks, stick suddenly devastating the stranded petal of a grave flower. The movies, on the other hand, are different. Everything is different in the movies. A novel is a meagre imitation of life compared to film's abilities. Film doesn't need to see the world humanly. Film doesn't need either your perspective or mine, or even necessarily that of any of its inhabitants. In a movie, the camera sees. The camera sees what I, you, Doug cannot see. This is an excellent argument for chemical perception, Doug thinks. The very fact that Doug thinks with a stick makes him characteristically kinomatic, which is a word he heard and appropriated at one of the monthly Film Society gatherings in Livery Street.

The puddle at the base of the gravestone on which Doug is seated has nothing to do with the bab but is instead an indication of the fact that the heavens have opened. The rain is gentle. The rain sloppy-snogs the stones of the cathedral, oiling them as opposed to cleaning them, but apart from that it is unobtrusive. It has taken Doug five minutes at least to notice it.

It's arguably rare for anyone, ever, to register a change in their environment perfectly instantly. To be able to do so would surely take all the fun out of it, perception. There is always a lag, a drag, between the world and the world as we know it. Doug's previous noticing of the Grand's glasslessness, for example, has only just now taken on significance, because at this point in the course of his musings Doug peeps upwards to discover that the windows of the Grand have glass in them.

The windows of the Grand now have glass of them. Before, they didn't.

Now *that*, Doug thinks, is a tad on the strange side.

He blinks twice, snaps his spine into position and has another gander.

The windows of the Grand have glass in them.

Now *that*, decides Doug, is impossible. How long has his bum been roosting on a miniature gravestone? How long has he been sat here failing to cerebrate the glitch of his meatlessness? For how long has been sat here being characterful? It's all becoming, Doug thinks, his stick now sturdying itself to bear the whole weight of him, far too confusing. But just as he is about to raise himself from the midget Margaretta's stele and map a vector either in the direction of 140 (to a disappointed Lotte) or else to the butcher's, he finds himself again observing the Grand's miraculously transmogrified upper stories. Then slowly lowering his gaze to the lowest of them, the storey that ever since the Grand's construction has contained a row of comely shops and is home to Crowan's the gentlemen's outfitters and Galloway the chemist, Doug comes across a series of words that commences with

NEXT

followed by

SAFEWAY

— all of which undoes Doug so much that he nearly wets both himself and Margaretta's memory. The safe way to what, exactly? Then Doug sees that to the left of the S A F E W A Y are still more words. Equally inexplicable, these ones promise

FREELANDINCANADA

even though Doug is pretty certain that all that kind of stuff ended yonks ago. Doug had an uncle who emigrated to Canada. The uncle's name was Stephan. Uncle Stephan was always flying low in the trouser department, as Doug remembers.

The rain quickens. The ground becomes visibly skiddier. Doug, who is not, he tries to remind himself, the type to leap to brash conclusions, and who doesn't believe in a god capable of inflicting upon Doug some terrible mental disease as retribution for Doug's flambé-ing of the familial farmhouse — this same Doug now maintains his hovering position above Margaretta's gravestone. The cathedral bells have started clanging in a rhythm distinctly experimental. The pigeons have hauled their hulks and scarpered, when usually Doug has no choice but to dispense of them forcibly. The air feels to Doug as if it is being wrested in two, a torn curtain. Like blancmange, time for Doug is congealing into a quivering assemblage of trembles. The figure who only moments ago was so nonchalantly crossing the cemetery, severed toilet bowl in tow, is back again. For some reason the toilet bowl figure has placed their fizzog extremely close to Doug's and started to contort it into constellations of expressions of what Doug interprets as i) horror, ii) concern and iii) exasperated impatience. Doug initially feels inclined to applaud this performance, but very quickly he wishes the figure would leave him alone to his private madness, which is what Doug now concludes has crashed into his cranium catastrophically, and which he is trying his best to fend off by composing the story of Doug's own life, or 'Doug: The Movie.' He'll miss out the boring bits and make them wait for the best bits, obviously.

REDEVELOPMENT

BI5

'Last night', the ww writes in her diary, 'Last night I went sleepwalking. Zero wasn't with me. I was alone, zonked, sleepwalking. I have scratches on my soles to prove that what I dreamt of, I really moved through. I really did: my brain is sudorific with the memory.

'In bed, at night, I wear one of Zero's old t-shirts, a rag that from the neck down collapses over all of me except my forearms, wrists, calves, shins, and ankles. I have shallow feet, thin ankles. I don't wear bedsocks, and I don't own any slippers. Slippers are for idiots: in slippers you never go forwards; all you can do is drag against the shag as if you were treading water. I have hard worn skin on my heels and I don't mind them getting dirty. Stony beaches have never hurt me. I did the long jump barefoot. The cindertrack felt amazing barefoot, especially when the sun was cooking it. In our bathroom we have a pummel-stone — it sits in the soapdish next to the toebrush — but I've never used it voluntarily. I want the hard skin on my heels to stay hard. Feet shouldn't slap the ground like fish. Feet should *smack* the ground, even if they don't stay there.

'The world I move through when I sleepwalk is the same world as this one, only nudged a bit. Zero doesn't believe me when I tell him. There's this small gap, I tell him, that you squeeze yourself into, and in that gap, things are themselves but at the same time not quite. Zero doesn't believe that I could really squeeze as far into that gap as I say I do. He has never come across me, eyes sparkling but unseeing, although when I say this to him he grins and says that that is how I seem to him most of the time, anyroad. Fair enough. I can be distant. He can be too. There is something incredibly clear and breathable about the air that slides between us.

'In the world I move through when I sleepwalk, the doorhandle is an ovenknob and an ovenknob is a doorhandle. Outside, if I get there, a dustbin is a postbox and a postbox is a dustbin.

'If I make it outside the house, the objects that switch with each other don't necessarily remain in the same scale as each other. In my room and in the house, the distance between the things and the things they switch into is usually very little. Outside, when it's dark enough for the sky to swallow itself, when the lid of the world lifts off like the lid of a toiletbowl and the stars squeak at the shit that's inside, then things swap between each other between greater distances: consistencies travel greater distances. Gravel beneath my toes and between them is gigantic sand and I am shrunken, a dot, one dimensional. Or I wade through concrete then get stuck in it. Then I am buried in it, the concrete, or it is as fine and weightless as snow and I make shapes in it. All of these things have happened. It's what happens when I sleepwalk.

'The wind can be a machine farting. A tree branch crackling is a window smashing. The road is a road but not our one. It goes somewhere else at the same time as going where it goes as well as going nowhere even though that's logically impossible unless your mechanics is quantum. Ten thousand cars rip along it. Then the road hasn't even been built yet. The road is a rough and tumble of smaller, skinnier roads studded with smaller, skinner houses and I bump into them, those houses, and their bricks and mortar graze my forrid. The road is woven with bushes and foxgloves and cat nip, and a puddle I put my bare foot in is the cut, the canal, and the lamp-post I smash my front teeth on is a concrete stilt ripping up from the mud and veering into the sky, a sky now scratched by sparks coming off the great construction site that what is beneath it has turned into. And then for the few moments I cling to the lamp-post, sickened by the impact of hitting it, I am no longer human: I am the concrete column's formwork, which is the 'temporary timbering or metalwork used for casting of concrete *in situ*', also called 'shuttering' or 'falsework.' That's what I am: the 'falsework.' I am what moulds the concrete lamp-post. I make it stay like that but I myself do not stay like that. Everything recedes into what it isn't and there it stays, swimming in itself, delirious. And then if I make it all the way from our row of ridiculous cottages to the new tower blocks they are still building — if I get there then the cut is full of pondfish. A washing line lacerates me. The hand that reaches out for me isn't my mom's but the mom of someone else's.'

CONVALESCENCE

B24

"It's as bad for you as smoking. It's bad for the environment." St. John hated driving as much as he hated people who smoked. It was definitely *people* who smoked whom St. John hated, not smoking *per se*, because once when Indy's dad had been standing at the Worlds End gates waiting to pick her up at the same time as St. John had been waiting there to pick up me, St. John had refused to greet Indy's dad, even to recognise him, because Indy's dad was smoking. St. John claimed that he simply *hadn't* recognised him and that was all, there was nothing more to it. But it wasn't true. I had seen St. John churn his gob and then spit on the weedy pavement. Indy's dad had had an embarrassed, shivery look about him. His eyelids fluttered after us disbelievingly as we passed him. The hand holding his cigarette went limp and dropped the cigarette. That was when I swore one day to take up smoking.

"I don't know why I did it. I just did it. OK?" We had picked my mom up from NEXT because something not nice had happened to her there, something to do with a delivery it had been her responsibility to deal with and a skip in the shop's basement. From what I could tell, she wasn't physically hurt or anything. We weren't on our way to the doctors. We had come down the corkscrew ramp of the multistorey car park that backed on to the shopping centre where NEXT was and driven out onto the road that swung away from the street that led to the doctors. Now we were waiting at traffic lights. Even more than he hated moving in a motorcar, St. John hated sitting waiting in one at traffic lights.

"Why don't you go the quick way?" Tacked to the post of the traffic lights was a printed notice alerting housewives to all the money they could earn without even leaving the house, ever. The notice had got soggy in the rain. Ink had split up into rainbows. I blinked at the notice and tried to memorise the telephone number.

"The quick way isn't the quick way. It takes longer in the end." St. John's eyes went into the mirror. I couldn't tell if he was looking at me or the road behind me.

"The quick way is definitely quicker."

I couldn't tell if he was looking at me or the road behind me.

PRECIPITATION

BI IBB

To the bab the map is a mirror. Its messiness is her messiness. In its red splotches she sees the blood that spurts through, and now from, herself. The bab's 'period', which for three whole years didn't come, not once, is suddenly sprawling all over her knickers, her pajama bottoms, the skirt she put on the first morning without realising what had occurred. The undersheet on her thin single bed is stained. Her stomach lurches. It's unexpected, this sudden return of womanhood. The bab had become accustomed to not having to worry about being prepared. For the best part of a week the bab has been staring into this map of hers in Eden as if to ask it: why I am bloody well bleeding now? What have I done? What have *you* done? The map never answers her back. It's so frustrating that it's tempting to take the muck in her gusset and sprawl it over the Enquiry Office walls. It's tempting to let the blood that gets stuck in her cuticles when she goes to 'the ladies' stay stuck, to stop clearing up what can never *ever* be cleared up. It's all confused, the map and the bab, the bab's 'womanly business', as it's called, and her work on the map. The map isn't a mirror at all. The map is barely recognisably a map anymore.

To begin with the idea worked well. The bab sat at her steel-legged desk feeling steely herself; the map was held down at the corners by pumice stone, a bag of sand, and a piece of white chalk; the bab sharpened her pencils and patiently awaited the incoming reports. Her mornings were poignant but perfunctory. Her toes went untouched by the nicks of glass that pinned themselves to her stilettos on her way from the cemetery to Eden. It was straightforward enough, once the latest in the line of visitors to reach the front of the queue had finished speaking, and weeping, and picking at the blood blisters pimpling their fingers — it was straightforward enough for the bab then to locate the correct co-ordinates and pin-point the plot with a neat cross, an action that had its piratical pleasures in spite of the gist of dreadfulness. The bombs buried the treasures and the bab recorded their burial: railway stations and gymnasiums; rubber plants and chemical labs; watch workshops and nib fakterois[1]; churches, religious houses, synagogues; cinemas and swimming pools; sinks, baths, toiletbowls; socks, bow-ties, pickled umbilical cords; buckles; 'Family Bibles' in the back pages of which were recorded generations of Clutterbucks, or whatever; Family

---

[1] Olsy worked in a pen nib fackteroi for a short time. She got the gig there after she got pregnant by the unknown soldier but before she found out she was. It was because of this gig that Olsy was able to depart from the family home, or 'hostel' as she then called it, at 140 Armoury Road. On the pen nib fackteroi floor, Olsy was what is called a 'marker'. To get a job in this line of work when bombs are falling like cats and dogs and when you are (or at least your body is) gearing up to give birth and when the Bíró brothers are about to run off to Argentina and patent their invention of the ballpoint is ironic to say the least, ar.

Health Encyclopedias; wads of cash and sacks of jewelry; centenary teaspoons and tiny swords; even the dolly mixtures (the sweets, not the 'pics') a child had brought the day before the fall of one bomb and stored in a stash out of sight of their mom; even mom's tiny treasure themselves. It was easy enough, at first. The exactness was satisfying. The bab kept her pencils and crayons insanely sharp. Cool, crimson, smooth, beardless, Humphrey B. Manzino had given the bab his detailed instructions and then left her to it, and the bab, crimson, smooth, beardless and cool, a total woebegone at art at school, set out to do her boss proud.

In the cabinets that dress the rear wall of the Enquiry Office she had found two cardboard boxes containing a store of carefully packed draughting instruments. The store included: i) the pencils B3 makes so much fun of; ii) two compasses; iii) something the bab has no idea what it's called but which she nonetheless makes good use of (it's a *spline*, and the bab rightly uses it for constructing curves); iv) a single 'set square.'

To the side of the sandbag and pumice stone, the items that press down the right side of the map, each instrument now has its position on the leathery top of the bab's desk. The set square is especially prominent. When the bab first found it she leant it casually against one desk leg, out of the way of her work on the map yet under threat of being toppled by a visitor if their gestures were especially 'expressive.' These days the set square rests at her elbow. The two compasses sit above it. The splice finds itself either aligned with one of the long sides of the map's rectangle, or balanced on the bab's thigh-flesh.

In the bab's mind all these instruments are objects once used by the *other*. That they were in his hands once, the bab is certain. His fingers manipulated them. His mouth made lovely vowel sounds when the compass cut a perfect circle. By handling the *other*'s instruments, the bab herself passed through the hands of the *other*.

Back when the bombs were first beginning to fall, when their roars were still awful and the gaps between them still had meaning, the bab's map-work had a way of making everything easier to cope with. The bombs fell. The bab kept a detailed record. The bab, in effect, kept a grip on the bombs. If it was possible to keep the bombs in place, more or less, then it was possible to keep everything else in place too, the past and the future included. But it didn't work that way for long. The map soon became messy, and the worst thing was that it was the detail, the bab's dedication and rigour, that *made* it messy. The more the bab worked, the more her work messed the map up. It wasn't even as if the map had anything to do with her finding her sister, Olsy. It wasn't helpful in that way whatsoever.

Olsy once said something to the bab that horrified her. It horrified her because the bab found it at once unimaginable and painfully possible. It had to do with the bab's true reasons for being with the *other*.

The bab, by the way, has never gotten around to giving the map a title. The map is simply and straightforwardly 'the map.' Those are the two words that the bab, with the aid of the *other*'s technical stencils, has inscribed at the top of the sheet of paper that with only a thin blank border contains the map. "How's the map?" is what B3 and everybody else who knows about it asks her. The map isn't known by anything else. The bab sometimes wishes Humphrey would provide an official title, something supple on the tongue while simultaneously sturdy enough to put anybody off properly interpreting it, or something purely numeric, or even something written out in shorthand. But it doesn't seem as if he intends to. All Manzino seems to do these days is stand upright at his fireplace, staring into the coals and the curling petals of burned paper. In those tiny firestorms, the bab supposes, he spies the future. In the fires that no chimney can channel — in the damage that the bab daily sketches — in those fires he spies the future likewise. Despite his hair sticking up at odd angles, Manzino is calm, dignified. Just as the bab is becoming nothing but a horrible wobble, at this time of relentless bombfall, bombshell older sisters and endless queues around Eden (the bab's visitors curl the walls), the boss, Humphrey, Manzino, Humphrey B. Manzino, is become a monument to incomparable patience. Whether 'patience' in this context should be read as 'calm yet courageous forbearance' or as 'sneaky determination' is not something the bab can be bothered to cogitate. It simply flusters the bab enormously. She hides in the toilet cubicle on Tuesdays.

It's not the blood that bothers her. It's the blood's

displacement, the way it gets everywhere. Olsy would no doubt tell her that that's what blood *is*, though: blood is not binding; blood is disruption.

The bab has by now been staring into her creation for so long and from so many angles (sometimes she steers the map round to take better aim at a certain circle, or else she steers herself around it the better to find a street already submerged in discharge) to notice that the nominal moniker she has given it, i.e., 'the map', is not all that far from her own moniker, i.e. 'the bab.' The map is the bab is the bam. The bam is the bab is the map. The map is a mess. The bab is a mess. B3 knows very well that she stays on in Eden well past working hours, but he never urges her to go home. He nods goodnight, pats down his bowler, smirks (the bab feels certain) about something that is *not* happening (for example, the bab and Humphrey) and is off. B15 is still around but barely talks. He barely uses his mouth even. The spam sandwiches are a thing of the past. The bab remains in the Enquiry Office alone, the sun sinking in Eden's windows, the boss's burbling snores sneaking through the walls, the compass metal chinking against the desk legs as the bab swings a weary hand, slumps.

Humphrey's small flirtations (the notes he stowed in her inkwell, or slipped between two fig rolls) turned out not to be flirtations at all.

What?

The map's a mess. The things that should give it its meaning, these things no longer even *show* on it. The alleyways, churches, synagogues, ODEONs and swimming pools are sunk, censored, obscured. Even the map's original grid is hard to decipher beneath the blobs by which the bab represents the bombs. They have swarmed, smeared, sprawled, fattened themselves up on each other's blood. The key the bab kept to begin with is a nursery rhyme now. It's impossible to tell from the layers of pencil and crayon whether the destruction the bab's marks refer to means that all that now remains is mud, the sandstone ridge the city sits upon re-erupted from the broken ground, or whether the destruction is such that buildings, bricks, a babba's dispersed rattle, etc., still survive. The bab herself no longer knows. The more attentive she tried to be, the more chaotic the map became. The more thorough she was in making her markings, the more the map blurred. The map blurred so much that it began to look as if the suburbs had turned back into fields, fields that had been flooded with blood. The bab no longer attempts to represent the number of buildings damaged or destroyed by each bomb by the specific circumference of a circle. Her notes are themselves so sub-sub-categorized she no longer knows where to find something, or what she will find where.

Here is how she began subdividing the damage done to buildings:

i) dwelling houses (including broken glass only)
ii) dwelling houses (seriously damaged)
iii) public buildings (including churches and religious

houses)

iv) business premises

v) *other*

The bab gets a crashing feeling every time her eyes cross that last *other*, but what can she do about it?

Here is how she divvies-up the damage done to people:

killed

seriously injured

slightly injured

The difficulty of ascertaining this kind of information from her queue of visitors is huge. Crude, too. It makes the bab's eyeballs singe and her stomach hurt all the more. If she does succeed in teasing an accurate account of the destruction from a mom who is no longer a mom, or a kid who is no longer much interested in fizgigs and things that go frigambob, there still remains the problem of working out what do with that account. The more accurate information the bab attempts to incorporate into the map the more the map ridicules the notion of accuracy. Is she supposed to amalgamate information about buildings with information about infrastructure? Should she integrate the information about infrastructure with information about people? Or is she supposed to keep all these things separate? But then if she attempts to keep things separate, the map quickly becomes inaccurate. There are small circles where there should be big ones. There is the suggestion that three people have died but that the buildings they died in are still alive, still standing, still roofed over with slate tiles, still entered into via blue painted doors and doormats exclaiming WELCOME. The bab does not know what to do. Humphrey's initial instructions have become useless. Does he not have more? And why is she bleeding now?

Three years ago the bab's periods stopped. It wasn't particularly unexpected and it wasn't particularly scary, since it wasn't exactly as if her periods had ever been very regular anyroad. B3 would no doubt have joked, had he known, that the bab had never been a *regular woman* at all. There were none amongst the other women of 140 Armoury Road who could sympathise or advise. The bab's mom had never had a spot of blood out of place or out of time. Her sister Olsy wore a new blouse on the day her periods started, said that when a woman was on her period she gave off special chemicals, evidently (the bab presumes) got pregnant very easily. The bab by contrast never believed she had it in her, 'it' being the ability to bleed on cue, to brew eggs and then evacuate them, to flex and squeeze her fallopian tubes like a man rippling his biceps. Either the bab was right to sense she would never be a *regular woman,* or she willed her body not to be. The bab isn't sure.

She does think this, though: that something in her was for some reason resisting all along, that her not having periods for three years was not simply a malfunction of her feminine organs, if that's what they're best called, but rather some kind of *statement* about the nature of those organs in the first place, what they meant to begin with at all. It seemed to the bab — though God knows when or how the seeming solidified into an actual thought — that men (and her mom) simply took it for granted that each month on the dot a woman got on with her bleeding, that she just did it, it simply happened, and she didn't have to think about one jot. It was as if the bab had made the discovery that *eigentlich* you do and don't have to think about it, this bleeding you're supposed, monthly, to perform.

What?

But then so why is she bleeding now? What has it got to do with the map? Why does she associate *that* with the muck in her gusset?

The bab doesn't know. Eden's walls don't know either, no matter how much the bab stares at them. B3 increasingly leaves her alone; even his lack of a sense of humour has been exhausted. The bab for her part is content to be left. Hanging around her almost constantly now is that atmosphere of compact solitude the toilet cubicle at the end of the row in 'the ladies' so helps to concentrate. Olsy is about to explode. The *other* never writes, or at least the bab doesn't get his letters. The world is expanding and contracting, expanding and contracting at the same time; the bab's map is there to show how it does so. From the day they started growing, the bab's bosoms, as her mom called them, were bruised all over; blue streaks strobed across them. No bomb has bashed the bab or slapped her with its turbulence. No shrapnel has bitten her thigh-flesh. 140 Armoury Road escaped destruction when the house three doors down was bombed out: buildings these days blink and are gone. Olsy is a bombshell yet to be dropped. How is she going to look after the child. How is she going to *give birth*. There is an elephant in every single room the bab walks into. The bab herself hasn't come to any harm. And yet this, itself, feels like harm.

B3

What is Doug?

    Doug is dead.

    Surely. He must be.

    What else could all this dirt mean? The beetle eating his eye out? The soil sweating into his bones and stuffing into his broken mouth?

    What is Doug?

    Doug is dead.

    It's certain. He must be.

    See, the screen has died. The screen is borderless now. There is no frill, no neon. There are no velvet red curtains. The screen is blank. The soil is screen. The beetle is screen.

    Where is Doug?

    Doug is buried. Doug is under. Doug is not Doug.

    Doug rolls. It hurts him to roll: there isn't one bit of him, it seems, that isn't bruised, as tender as a tenderized steak slab. But then the fact that he *can* roll is both reassuring and confusing.

    Where was Doug?

    He was perched above a gravestone. Now he is beneath one. Enwombed, entombed. Doug is in a cinema and the film has finished, obviously. There is a voice somewhere around him, but it's as soft as the soil in his mouth and as blank as the borderless screen now surrounding him. But Doug does not hear voices at the bottom of an aristotle of whiskey. His clothes do not become crumpled when he has been drinking. Even when he cannot stand up straight, Doug does not hear voices. There are no fairies at the end of the garden. There is no getting to the other side of the rainbow.

Is it possible that Doug is not not? That Doug is not not Doug?

Never.

The voice in the near distance is getting bigger and beginning to glow a bit.

"Doug."

"..."

"Doug!"

Doug rolls again. Everything hurts again.

"Yes, Doug's my name."

The voice briefly becomes a rumble. It dawns on Doug that the rumbling is laughter. He snaps his dead eyes open. The screen remains borderless, but even without being able to see them, or anything with them, Doug can tell his eyes are working.

That's strange, Doug thinks. Is this what death is then?

"Yes! Doug's my name. Could you be so good as to tell me where my stick is?"

The voice is silent. At the unthinkable thought of being stickless, Doug shudders. His mouth, on the other hand, has something pleasant rushing through it. Doug gulps at whatever it is. A few seconds later the rushing ceases. The taste of condensed sky remains resting on his tongue for a while afterwards.

"Water."

"Yes, sort of."

"Thanks!"

"Not at all."

"No, really. Thanks!"

Gradually, as he becomes accustomed to the strangeness, Doug tests his senses. Having ascertained the functioning of his irises and tastebuds — even if he is yet to see anything, and even if it is only tastelessness he has so far tasted — he moves on to examining the abilities of his dead nostrils, which in life were prodigious. Doug sniffs. Doug smells nothingness in all its nauseating savagery: collapse, stagnation, destruction. The smell smells terrible. Doug spits. The stuff he spits is grizzly. Not that Doug has ever tasted such a substance, but what he spits tastes to him like afterbirth.

"It stinks."

"Safe, though!"

It comes to Doug that his feet are freezing. How strange feet are! So far away, and yet so essential! Doug smiles. Doug stops smiling. That last word said by the voice, which seems small and close by at the same time, has reminded him of something.

"Safe?"

"Safe, sir."

"Next?"

"Not quite what you'd call the next life, sir, but nearly, yes."

REDEVELOPMENT

BI5

In days leading up to Zero's gig, the ww succumbs to the bab's cajoling and again stays at home to recover — to sweat out the feverish sweatiness that 'sweating it out' brought on in her, and this time properly. There is nothing tangible for her to recover from, though. The fever, if fever it was, was a weird one: the ww felt fine for most of it and doesn't know when it began; surely it wasn't that smear of rain that snuck down her collar. Her period, which is on at the moment, is collapsing out of her in spasms, but she's used to that. That can't be it. The only thing the ww can put a finger on is the metallic taste of her tiredness, a tiredness that is the opposite of sleepiness and that slices right through her eyeballs: a tiredness that pierces her irises like shrapnel. It doesn't help that she has started to sleepwalk again. At night, she either fidgets without sleeping, or she sleepwalks.

The days she spends at home are boring. Long. Taut. Scrappy. Boring. In their tiredness her eyeballs have grown sinewy: she spends a fair amount of time pressing the flesh beneath them till the flesh crackles. Her head she leaves resting on the towels in the airing cupboard for longer and longer intervals. Dressing-gowned but forever unslippered, the ww takes to swapping between her parent's room — the room in which she discovered her birth certificate — and the empty rear bedroom at the back of the semi-detached cottage, the room she's never got around to moving in to. From her parents' room there is the view, still not totally smothered with foliage, of the new tower blocks in the distance, the ones her so-called dad was overseeing when he was still working. The tower blocks tease the sky like unlaunched space rockets. Up to their base sneak rows of tunnelbacks: some of the chimneys still smoke, some don't. The tower blocks tower over the tunnelbacks as a row of dominoes does a set of splayed fingers. The boxy windows are what most foreign languages are to the ww: hieroglyphics. The ww can't see anything in them. Space rockets, dominoes, stone tablets: the ww doesn't really know what she thinks of the tower blocks. Increasingly they simply appear to her as incomplete tower blocks. They've been standing unfinished for months now. The *other* never mentions them, but then he barely mentions anything. From the rear window, the ww watches him filling in the well that has fallen in on itself in the flowery back garden. The well re-opened of its own accord. A cat, a tabby that belongs to the neighbours, fell into the well and got stuck along with the bab. The cat's paws were orange-freckled, same as the ww's pale fizzog.

These are the kind of things the ww now sees and thinks about.

The ww yawns, wipes her mouth on the sleeve of her dressing gown, throws herself down on the bed, belly upwards, remembers saying:

"Tell me."

The bab stepped forward. The apron she was wearing was frilly.

"Olsy."

"Olsy is. Or Olsy was?"

"Is."

"..."

"..."

"Do you know where she lives?"

"..."

"..."

"Sounds like 'ulcer.'"

"I beg your pardon."

"Olsy. It sounds like 'ulcer.'"

"..."

"..."

"I could write down the address for you."

"You have the address?"

"Yes. I do."

"Have you had it always?"

"No. Not always."

The ww has recently returned to the pages of *Fowler's* and *A Concise Building Encyclopedia*. Her work lacks any method whatsoever now, and, for no good reason other than the pleasure she takes in sitting back and reflecting about the free-floating small metal items suspended in space, mid-explosion, she combines her glances at *Fowler's* with copying out 'exploded diagrams' of kitchen appliances. The things that attract her attention in *Fowler's* and the *Encyclopedia* now are: i) The 'jib' of a derrick crane. 'Jib, jib jib, jab, jab, jab, jib, jib, jib.' (The is what the ww spends an hour or so saying nothing much but); ii) The various kinds of arches, whether *stilted* or *inverted* or *parabolic* or *rampant*. The ww wonders what kind of arch she would be. Inverted? Rampant? iii) The 'Theodolite', which is a 'telescopic instrument used in surveying for measuring angles, either vertically or horizontally.' The ww briefly wonders whether the *other* has one somewhere, but can't be bothered to ask him.

The days are boring. Long. Taut. Boring.

The exploded diagram she spends the most time on is one of the electric washing machine, a single tub washing machine which, like the refrigerator, is a relatively new phenomenon in the ww's household. The ww takes pleasure in individually sketching the many varied screws that hold together the washing machine.

The days are boring. Then it's Saturday. For the first time since she has last seen him, the ww slips out of Zero's old t-shirt, shuns the dressing-gown drowsily hanging on a peg in the bathroom, and steps into a pair of tight trousers. Her wrist is still twitching with the watch she never looks at.

Then the ww goes downstairs and makes an announcement.

"I'm going to Zero's gig tonight. Then I'm going to

work on a construction site. If you really want to know it's what a really amazing female philosopher once did."

To the ww's surprise, the bab doesn't stop stuffing washing into the washing machine.

In desperation the ww adds a far from desperate (in her opinion) detail.

"She was French. Like Rambo."

The *other* isn't inside to stop what he's doing and look up, startled. He's doing what he's been doing ever since the well fell in on itself. He's working on the well. Tool sounds come mutedly through the scullery window. He's fiddling with the well. He isn't fixing it. He's fiddling it. Fiddle. Clack. Hollowed sounds coming from a hollowed man. The sun snags on a trowel then skids into the *other*'s glasses. His miniature construction site gets reflected in the glasses. Why make such a fuss about it? Why not just fill the well in with concrete? That would be much easier than whatever it is the *other* is doing.

This is what the ww thinks.

The bab's bum shudders when she bends over to pick up more washing. The scrape of the clothes going into the drum is punctured by the scrapes coming in from the other side of the window, where the *other* works. Then the door opens, and the *other* is standing there. He shoots an arm out to a shelf, extracts a pencil from a pencil pot, slots the pencil behind one waggy ear, exits.

The ww gawps at the world's indifference, astonished. Then out of nothing the bab starts talking. Her hair is still pinned up in last night's rollers.The world slips out of the ww's grip like a pair of scissors. The ww winces, but the bab continues talking, stuffing the drum with soiled clothes, talking. Beyond the windowpane, the well worker continues tinkering.

"Sounds like 'ulcer.'"

The bab's eyes burn at the ww. Whatever mettle the ww still has in her, rusts immediately.

"What?"

The ww gulps.

"'Olsy.' It sounds like 'ulcer.'"

The bab's lips lessen in thickness a bit.

"OK."

"Soz."

"It's OK."

"OK."

"My parents had a boarding house in Lozells not far from your school."

"I know."

"Your granddad died in a cemetery."

"I know."

"Olsy was fabulous."

"You said."

"Frank —"

"Frank?"

"Your uncle. He died."

"Like Doug."

"Yes. But Doug died here."

The bab pauses, presses a big yellow button on the washing machine, waits for the revelations to begin, resumes. The onset of the machine's slow churning sounds settles the ww down a bit.

"Before I moved out, Olsy and I shared a small room together. It was barely bigger than the airing cupboard in this house. Well, that's an exaggeration I suppose, but it was small. There was only a slit of a window in it. Through the walls we could hear the boarders moving in *their* rooms. We could hear their taps chortling water. If we put a glass to the wall we could hear them snoring. Sometimes we could hear the snores without putting a glass to wall. There'd be a rattle in our little window if the snores were strong enough."

For the first time ever it occurs to the ww that her mom has never given birth to anybody. Unless there is a version of her, the ww, somewhere, shifted onto another sister somewhere. But what difference would that make? To all the momentous realisations the ww has been having recently the ww is now adding this one: no realisation in the world could ever be momentous enough to satisfy her. Life is low drama. This is what the ww thinks.

The bab meanwhile breathes wearily. Her eyes stoop back to the emptied washing tub, blink at it tinnily. To her side the full metal drum has segued to another kind of whirring sound. The ww recognises this as the second segment of the machine's cycle. The revolutions continue.

"In Olsy's head boarding houses and brothels were

associated."

"They both begin with 'b'."

"They do."

"..."

"Doug said she was 'fermenting'. He would say that. He was what people called a character. He hated novels. He loved movies. He loved going to the cinema. He founded a film society. I used to meet him for lunch in the ODEON. He said that the movies weren't about characters, that movies captured something about people that was less together, less gathered."

"..."

"Doug was killed in the bombs."

"I know."

"In the cemetery. I had to mark the spot on my map."

"It's quite funny."

"Yes."

"What map?"

"Olsy wanted to get out of there. The men — our boarding house was men only — the men all thought we were maids, which we were in effect. I was better at school than Olsy. Or at least, I worked harder. I went to the college and got my secretarial certificate. Learned to touch-type and do shorthand. I *adored* doing shorthand. Then I went for an interview with the Corporation and there were rows and rows of typewriters, each one set at its own small table. Next to the typewriters were pads of paper and a pencil. For the shorthand test. I was so nervous I stabbed myself with the pencil. I still have the mark it made on my hand. Here."

The bab extends an upturned palm in the ww's direction. From where she is standing the ww can't make out any kind of mark on it. Tinkles and taps stab at the gurgle of the washing machine. The ww looks back out to the *other*, still working at the well.

"A shock of blonde."

"That's how we said it, yes. Well, Doug's death must have got to her I think. We said, "she has sent us all to Coventry.""

"Concrete."

The word pops out of the ww's mouth involuntarily.

"What about it?"

"Nothing. Sorry. You were talking about Coventry."

"Only metaphorically. Haven't you heard that saying before?"

"No."

The bab gazes at the ww querulously, disappointment dropping out from her eyes like dung from the horse of a rag and bone man.

"Olsy sent us all to Coventry. I just mean she stopped talking to us. This was when I was working for the Corporation."

The most the ww can say is:

"Yes."

"On the map."

"*What map*, mom?"

The ww's heart skiffles. Frustrated, she scrapes a chair from the kitchen table and plonks herself down on it.

The bab continues:

"I had to make a mark where every single bomb fell. That was my job. I worked in the office of the City Surveyor and Engineer. In Eden."

"Eden."

"Yes."

They both look out at the *other*, working. For every 'well' the bab has spoken, said in order to stall what she is saying for a second, the *other* has tinkered with the well that collapsed of its own accord in their garden and into which the bab fell. The *other*, in other words, has attempted to fill the hole in his own way. This is what the ww thinks.

The bab comes over to the ww, sits down beside her.

The ww wiggles her ears, says nothing, watches the *other*. The handkerchief covering the bald curve of scalp on his skull makes her giggle. The giggle scalds her chestbone.

"Ace, Zero."

"Ta."

"Ace. Really ace."

"Ta."

"Ace."

"..."

"So *cool*."

Zero is once more stood with a glistening beer can between his fingers. Elegantly slender as they are, the fingers wrap the can easily, sweepingly. The tips tap at the metal in runs of threes and runs of four. Then they stop and press down until there's a clap and the metal is dented. Two fingers caress the dent's ridges. Then the hand relaxes its squeeze. Then the tips resume their tapping.

This is what Zero does with a beer can when all that nervous energy has spun rhythms within him. This is what Zero does after a gig, basically.

In his spare hand, rested gently against his thigh-flesh, is his electric guitar. Its metal wires wetly twinkle. Zero himself is as sweaty as a fresh beer can. A fly darts onto his fagburn and settles, rubs its buggy eyes like a whining child does. Zero stares at it, disbelievingly. On the chest of his t-shirt a perfect circle burns to red, smolders.

It's the bar's lights, dancing.

Zero wouldn't hurt a fly.

The ww flicks the fly off for him.

"Ace, Zero."

Then the ww gives Zero two concise kisses: one on the cheek and one on the forrid. The raw tenderness of the second kiss — is it something to do with a forrid's forwardness that makes a quick peck there so exposing, so hopeless? — this tenderness shocks them both so that they keel a bit. The ww's lips have left a pulsing green mark behind them. Then the mark turns orange. Then the mark smashes into Zero's nose, staggers, skips off somewhere. The ww smirks. Under cover of the bar's bouncing lights, the two of them turn their eyes away from each other briefly. Then under cover of the bar's bouncing lights, their eyes clamber back into each other's. Their eyes clamber into each other's like two toddlers sneaking into a den they've built out of rags, pans and screwdrivers between the kitchen table and the windowledge. But the ww and Zero aren't in a den together. They're back in the basement of the bar that is not the K A R D O M A H.

Zero has just played a gig in there.

Bosting.

The soupy air around them hiccups. The basement is warm and sticky. The bands are all finished now. Zero's band was the last of three bands to play. The other two acts were a) three cropped boys from the grammar school opposite the ww's old one, one of whom the ww once slept with; b) a woman who extracted sonic wobbles from the air by making shapes with her hand by a radio antenna. The bands are all finished now but the ww's eardrums are still buzzing. From the massive speakers on each side of the stage a furry grumble is still coming, too. The speakers frame the ww and Zero, compress them. By their knees, which every now and again knock against each other, are more speakers; these are the monitors, the speakers the band hears but not the audience. Zero's monitor squats over a carefully assembled circuit of pedals, a series of connected boxes with small knobs on them. Cables stick out of the boxes' sides. The dinky red bulbs on one are still zapping around in a semi-circle — every now and then another set of dinky red bulbs on the same pedal shouts out a random character:

$$D\sharp, E, F\sharp, A\flat, E$$

This pedal is Zero's tuner: it's not in use now, but it's still chattering, checking wriggles of electricity for snippets of meaning. It's the only thing Zero is still to turn off. Zero himself is very quiet. He's always quiet after a gig.

The ww is trying to think of something else to say other than 'ace', or 'cool', or 'great'. Saying 'bosting' is difficult because saying it makes her feel like a plonker.

"Hey, you broke a string."

"Yeah."

"But it didn't matter."

Zero shrugs, snaps some beer back, thumbs a string

on the unplugged guitar. Except it's not a string. It's a wire, a wire that's been drawn until its diameter is exactly as fat as it should be, the right thickness or thinness exactly. That's the way Zero thinks about guitar strings. Zero draws wire to earn a living. He makes wire vibrate to feel better about the fact that drawing wire is how he earns a living.

"Nah."

"..."

"It didn't matter."

Zero spends his nights thrashing the wires he spends his daylight hours drawing, pulling, passing through a die.

Dying.

"..."

The soupy air struggles through the small gap between them.

The electric guitar isn't an instrument. It's a piece of machinery like any other. That's what Zero sees very clearly.

"..."

"I liked the second one. The last one was good too."

"Ta."

The ww screws up her nose, takes a sip of beer from her own can, enjoys the sizzle that spreads over her tongue. The ww is a bit drunk. The ww started drinking about two hours ago now, when Zero was soundchecking. The woman with the theremin bought the ww a whiskey.

Her eyeballs tottering, the ww stabs a finger into the red flare that's reappeared on Zero's chest.

"But I keep forgetting what you're *called*."

Zero blinks. What the ww has just said is one of those extraordinary blisterings of the ordinary world, when what one person says is received rightly in terms of its sound, but wrongly in terms of intention. Zero squeams, wipes some sweat from the rut between his nose and his upper lip.

"Zero."

"What?"

"..."

"The name of your band, you dope."

Zero laughs, relieved. The red flare on his chest bumps, then again vanishes.

"I meant the name of your *band*."

The ww's breath is as soupy as the basement air it sucks on. Zero doesn't mind. He likes the ww's skewifness. He likes it that she confuses him.

"We don't know yet. Can't agree on anything."

"Well, what have you have come up with?"

Zero drags hair from out of his eyes, shakes his head, smiles.

"They all sound crap as soon as I say them."

"Try me."

Zero pauses.

"Nah. Not now, like."

Handing his beer can to the ww, Zero bends to his pedals. Unbothered, the ww squats on the side of the stage, swigging alternately on her beer can and his. For no reason, she surreptitiously gobs a dollop of saliva into Zero's drink. Zero pops cables from a chorus pedal, a reverb pedal, coils the cables neatly, stacks the pedals in a rectangular briefcase with metal sides. The ww watches him, absorbed.

"Looks like you've got a bomb in there."

Zero ignores her, peers closely at the overdrive, prods a screw that seems to have come loose on it, shakes his head, stacks the pedal along with the others.

A girl comes stuttering up, stiletto-heeled, to congratulate Zero voluptuously. The ww simultaneously rubs her tummy and pats her scalp, which is the ww's way of saying that, while she knows what a polyrhythm is, that girl is stupid. The girl stutters off soon enough. Glowing, Zero turns to the ww, sticks his tongue out, winks at her.

"See yo, Zero."

It's the drummer of Zero's band, three huge drum bags burying him. Zero slaps his back, says something about the date of their next practice, adjusts one of the buckles on one of straps of the bags. The ww waves the drummer off, her arm arcing wildly and spraying a rainbow of beer behind it. The drummer's squashed totter makes her laugh. Zero looks to see what she is laughing at.

"Blotto."

The ww gasps in mock horror.

"Am not."

Zero wags his head, then returns to sorting his pedals. The ww rounds her mouth into an exaggerated yawn, bangs her unheeled feet against the stage.

"Come on, Zero. Aren't we supposed to be going somewhere?"

Zero's fingers are long and spindly but their pads are tough, reptilian. The tips have been worn hard by wires.

"Come on, Zero."

Up right by his eyes is Zero's left hand.

"Come on, Zero. They're all there."

The ww is up by his side, packing the last of his pedals for him, closing the pedal case. The bar's lights have at last stopped bouncing; harsh light has swallowed them. The glare reveals toppled chairs and ramshackle tables, squashed cigarette ends, a puddle of stickiness, compressed beer cans, a solitary glass of water perched on top of one of the tall speakers. The nasty smell sharpens suddenly. The ww donates two emptied cans to the demolition scene.

"Filthy. Let's go, shall we?"

When they get outside the blank air frightens them. The ooze moves along the tunnel that is New Street slowly, taking them with it then releasing them, then collecting them back up again into its grunge. In a while the ww and Zero find themselves standing under a streetlight near the old ODEON, opposite the Central Library. The buildings sink into the ooze sullenly. The ww winces, stamps her feet on the ground. Two things steer the ww's heart at this point (B3) in time (?): i) impatience (with Zero, with *this place*); and ii) true love (for Zero, for *this place, this shoddy city*).

"So, Zero, where are we going?"

It's difficult, discovering you're an oos-bird and because of this discovery simultaneously discovering that you would have been an oos-bird anyroad, even if you were not technically an oos-bird.

"A what?"

"Oos-bird."

"*Oos*-bird."

"That's what I am? That's what a bastard is? That's what we both are, then?"

The ww slumps against a broken gravestone. At some point, the stone has been snapped in two.

"Yo asked."

"True."

"But yo would have been one anyroad."

"What? A bastard?"

"An oos-bird."

"..."

"Is this it then? Is this where you're taking me? A cemetery? Excellent."

Zero grabs her hand, yanks it.

"Nah."

The ww's ears still have the rumble of Zero's afterbirth in them: this makes the night jangle.

"Oh, we're *here*. Near Eden. The road —"

But Zero has yanked her hand again. They go across the roadway, then for some reason back across it.

"Tinnitus."

"Tinn-i-tus."

The ww wiggles her ears as if trying to wiggle the tin inside them out.

"Come on."

"So who's in a hurry now?"

"Zero?"

" ..."

"Zero, do you think I should go see her? I've got the address. I've got it here with me now. Guess where she lives."

" ..."

"Zero? Guess where she lives!"

" ..."

"Ouch."

Into the night's ooze the moon is dribbling a trickle of foamy gob. The ww has caught herself on something and snagged her foot: on a brick, or else a coiled cable of some sort. The ww kicks back hard at whatever it is, violently.

"Where've you gone?"

The ww passes one dizzied hand through the dark. It reaches not Zero but a gap in a wall, or in a door. The gap is vomiting soggy paper. Then a beam of moongob illuminates a rotund postbox stuffed with rubbish and prostitutes' calling cards.

"It's a postbox!"

The ww laughs, drunk again all of a sudden. The beer

that sizzled first on her tongue and then in her heart is sizzling in her head now. Her ears sing along to the sizzle wheezily. One of Zero's chord structures is riffing through her repeatedly.

"..."

"Zero?"

Zero comes closer. A beam of moongob momentarily falls. He glints at the ww soberly. The ww straightens up, sobered. It's chilly now.

"Turbulence. Tinnitus. Turbulence."

"..."

Feeling a twinge of the fever she's just overgot, the ww rubs at her eyes like the fly that only a while ago landed on Zero's fagburn. The ww sighs, bristles, wishes they'd brought some more beers along.

"Where *are* we?"

Zero's right by her side again now. The ww grips a fist round his left arm to keep hold of him. Beneath her fingers, the contours of his fagburn feel firm, almost rigid. For some reason Zero doesn't like her holding him there. He undoes her grip quietly, with quick, expert digits. The ww doesn't notice the roughness of the fingerpads as they work at her. All she ever notices is the sore kiss of Zero's fagburn and how long Zero's fingers are.

"I thought yowed know."

"I can't *see* anything."

"..."

"Oh."

In the distance, sitting squatly on a peak above a riverbed of tubes, is the cabin where the ww met with the man who sent her off to sweat it out, the man in charge of building the city's new inner ring road. On the cabin's roof a rectangular red bulb throbs. It sends off enough slow radiance to throb its surroundings a dull red too. The moongob is useless now. All it can do is add a slight glitter to the circumference of the tubes. The tubes look like huge guitar leads, guitar leads for giant guitars.

The ww, nervous, laughs.

The cabin has moved since the ww's visit, just as the man said it would. The ww does not remember these tubes, the wrecked brick structures, this enormous steel frame that doesn't look like any building the ww has ever known. Unless it's just that whatever building the steel frame once was unrecognizable now. Unless the ww has never known any building like this steel frame will eventually become. The cabin wasn't sitting on a peak like that before. The hut is perched above a riverbed strewn with tubes. The riverbed zooms through a trench cut out of wrecked brick structures. The way it zooms makes it look as though this is land that elephants stampeded through, or else like a horizontal bomb screwed through the all buildings, bored a path, swung gradually round.

"This is the ring road. This is the inner ring road, Zero."

"This was Livery Street."

"Livery Street? Are you sure?"

"Ar."

The ww runs her eyes along his fingerline. Zero's pointing towards where the horizontality ends, where there are already columns and pillars, piers, the beginnings of a system of ramps. It's where the road will rise, overhang itself. It's a place Zero and the ww will return to a number of times over the next week. It's also the place where on their third visit — or maybe their fourth — they get caught, panting, pants down, the ww's upturned fizzog fried bright pink first by the cabin's red light and then by an angry torch and then — but it's too late to stop now.

~

'The resemblance between a spider's web and the arrangement of our city's roads is well known. The formation is that of a spiral orb. First, spoking out from the centre, come the radial roads, arterial routes whose pavements trace the old ways in and out of the city. Linking these roads at intervals, like the chords of a spider's trap, are those streets that once connected villages with farmsteads via fields fluffy with grain and turf. Today, those villages and farmsteads have been absorbed by the city, concreted and confused, and the streets that link them combine to form, around a central point, a series of concentric rings connecting suburban node to suburban node. Again, we need only think of the common cobweb, observable in any cellar, shed, or bedroom wardrobe, in order to picture this.

'The system has been described as 'sinuous.' It is supple, strong, and expandable, permitting coherent movement and discouraging congestion. And yet, in its present state our web is missing something. Whilst the pathways of both an outer and a middle ring can easily be discerned by bird and plane, there is, as of now, no inner ring to speak of. In the piecemeal evolution of the system, the innermost ring has been omitted. The central circle was leapfrogged: fatally ignored. In the interests of our city's future, it is exactly this gap, this apparent oversight, that the Corporation must set out to eradicate. That must be our work.'

Badly cut clipping.

~

CONVALESCENCE

B24

I was not born a mizzerling. I became one. I became one when I realised that my parents had a past that was not mine, a past that had nothing to do with me, but which was still with me. It was with me and without me, all about me but not *about me*. It, this past of theirs, stuck into every word that they didn't mean me to hear but which cracked against my flattened skull anyroad. St. John, especially, said nothing to me and, as far as I could tell, barely anything to my mom about his past wife. I knew she existed. But because St. John had rid all the cupboards in our house of any photographs of him and his past wife together — since St. John had shredded and shed his past wife completely the only image of her available to me was one I saw in a recurring dream. There was nothing in the dream that confirmed the woman I saw in it to be her, St. John's past wife. There was nothing in the waking world of B24 — if B24 ever woke from its own recurring dream — that spoke of her existence. Apart from the twins, of course. But even then I had a hard time putting all this together. The twins had a different mom to me, OK, but that figure did not easily match up in my mind with St. John's first wife. I didn't know her name, even. But the dream became her over and over. Her hair grew straighter each time I dreamt of it. Her smile grew more awful.

I felt bad for her in a way I had no way of understanding. I got into a car with the twin's mom and never got out again. I got into a car with her and did not realise for some time that she was not my mom. Then when I did I wanted to send my mom a letter explaining what had happened, but this other mom would not let me. There was nothing to explain, she said.

The past was all before me, but it was also *all before me*, waiting for me. It was a sleep out of which the world was slowly waking, or trying to, but which I was always on the brink of tripping over and/or collapsing into. The past was coming for me, coming to get me. I vividly saw what everything I watched on TV had *eigentlich* already taught me: that the past is an extraterrestrial, come back from the future.

Before y6, I had never been the kind to skip school. Even when I was ill, I still insisted on attending. The Tis'ers did their best to discourage epidemics of snotty noses and rancid earlobes, of stomachs overturning at short notice and of all that cognitive vomit becoming physical and slushing the Worlds End floors with pink custard or chocolate concrete. But however bad I felt, before y6, I always insisted on going in and passing my germs on. I would not go so far as to say I loved school, but I didn't hold myself against it in the way some of my classmates did.

It was only in y6 that I discovered in me a resistance; it was only in y6 that I discovered I could say no. That I could not go to school. That I could not.

I don't know whether it was the rain — I don't know

whether the rain really came. I remember the buckets and the blistering ceiling and feeling as if it had always been sunny up until then. I don't know whether it had anything to do with that term's project on the inner ring road, all the snippings and stories and curiosities that I assembled because of that project. I continued compiling my scrapbook, still very neatly, still very assiduously, even when there was no impetus, no ticks and no gold stars. St. John's title, *The Decline and Fall of the Inner Ring Road*, stayed around but got slightly sidelined: first it became the sub-title, then it was relegated to the sub-sub-title. This process mostly reflected the fact that I had discovered the double colon. Texts excerpted from newspapers collided with invented scenes, imaginary interviews, drawings, stories, some somewhat wild in places, though what do you expect from a y6er, even a clever one. When the document was finished I presented it to my mom, who read it cover to cover, then sobbed. I had said some not very nice and totally irrelevant things in it, but that these made her sob shocked me. I don't know. I don't know if it was to do with the deep religiosity that swelled in me and the disappointment of realising that not many people — not even the vicar — really took that kind of thing seriously, that really they thought religion was good for you up to a point and after that, a bit of a nuisance. I don't know how much it had to do with Worlds End itself. Y6 should have been my last year there. I left before it could leave me. Leaving something before something could leave me was a habit I got into before I had a good reason for doing so.

Anyroad. I discovered I could not go. There was no point in me announcing my presence by means of a breathless undigested

HERE!

because us y6ers shouting out our existence like that had nothing to do with the gridded register collected each morning from the office by whoever's turn it was. It had to do with the school trying to teach us to take responsibility for ourselves and for our whereabouts: for ourselves as having a whereabouts, as being locatable, discoverable, as being human beings who could convincingly give the impression that the ground was beneath them. They were trying to teach us to take a place in the world and then to stick to it. To take a place in the world and then be that place, become it. Be consistent with whatever position you once found yourself in one day. Be consistent with whatever position you found it so difficult to twist youself into even though you had never been in any other position.

In y6, I resisted. To begin with my mom was unconvinced. She set St. John, whose working hours were haphazard, on sentry duty. My nose poked through two banisters, I watched her blue coat bustle along the hall. I could see her padded shoulders in the mirror and I could hear the words they rose and fell with, but St. John was beyond me. He was watching TV in the living room.

"She's not really ill."

"…"

"She's not ill at all. I think she's fine."

"…"

"St. John, will you watch her please? She's not to get out of bed."

I tensed.

"Please, St. John."

"…"

"I'll be home by four. Goodbye."

"…"

I went back to my room and pulled open the curtains. The sun washed the walls and lifted the objects around me — splayed books and snapped pens, a barren piggy bank, some playground pogs — into life. I snatched the curtains back, so that life would not be able to live.

"What are you doing?"

He had come up the stairs and stared at me in silence.

"Your mom says you say you're ill. Are you ill?"

I opened the curtains and sat down in a trapezoid of light. He stayed standing in the doorframe, one hand tapping a corduroy trouser leg, the other tracing the outline of his moustache. His presence melted my actions into an obnoxious slush. I was not ill, but I was bothered. Snorts threatened my nostrils. I held them off.

"Are you feeling poorly?"

"No."

"You're not ill?"

"No."

He paused. I was looking at his slippers. They had some sort of insignia stitched into the top.

"I'm not ill."

"OK."

And then he switched on the electric light. Its beams were imperceptible: all that could really be seen was the struggling bulb. Obliterated electricity fell between my fingers. A moth popped into the room from nowhere. It looped the loop towards the shade and began beating itself up against the bulb. St. John and I both watched it for a while. Then I stood up and watched St. John. He looked at me at me like I'd looked at Watt when Watt had been sprawled dead on his wheel, and then, in the same way that I had fed Watt chips and chocolate fingers, he offered me one of his philosophical nuggets. He offered these out like peanuts.

"Like turning on the lights so as to see the dark."

"What?"

"Like turning on the lights so as to see the dark."

He nodded, mumbled nothing, and then went downstairs.

He went downstairs.

I stood there.

I can see the point of making a plan and sticking to it, but I've discovered that it's also necessary to be able to forgive yourself if and when the plan unsticks itself. The world tumbles through your fingers like obliterated electricity. For six days in a row you get up, brush your teeth, and get on with everything. On the seventh day you wake too early and get into a fisticuffs with the morning before the morning has even formed itself. Hence the invention of the Sabbath. Give time some slack. Let the wind ruffle your letterbox.

I stood there.

I went to bed that night.

I stood there. I went to bed at night.

Then it was the second Tuesday in a row that I should have been at Worlds End and wasn't. I woke early, even earlier than I would have done had I been planning on going to school, and couldn't return to sleepiness. I lay still and watched a sunbeam suck the dust off the bedside table. By the time the time had come to kick off the covers, a tiredness had crept into my eyes and made them hurt me. The sleep in my eyes hurt me.

I used to have trouble sleeping. I'd catch a glimpse of the world too early and not be able to stop myself from watching it. I would think about everything, about everyone. I squeezed my squint into the room's corners and discovered everybody I knew's abandoned marbles, what they'd said yesterday or yonks ago and also what they had never said. Then I span these thoughts around until they became magic balls foretelling events that were yet to happen, or events that would never happen, or events that would only happen because I had thought about them so much they *had* to. The walls in my bedroom, which were papered with woodchip, seemed to me to breathe heavily in the early morning. The walls were not well, somehow. I would run my fingers over the bumps and rub away at the layers of emulsion. In one wall, the wall my bed was up against, I thumbed a hole I would have worked all the way through to our neighbours' if my mom hadn't spotted it. It was something to hook my finger into and hold onto on one of the mornings when I woke up too early, or to hold onto across the Os and Ts and Es it took me to get to sleep in the first place. I was still then under the impression that the land of nod was a place it was possible to get to, a place you could spell the name of if only you concentrated on your oscarfizzog hard enough; either you got to sleep, or you fell there. There were also times when I woke in the middle of the night and didn't know where it was I had woken. St. John pointed out that this was not surprising. In B24, our houses looked all the more alike at night than they did in daylight. I could have been in anybody's bedroom.

But I knew where I was on this morning. I knew because I also knew, or thought I knew, where it was I was going. The night before I had made sure to inscribe the future in the objects around me, so that I would be certain, when I awoke, that the future had arrived and I was in it. There was Ted, sat expectantly at the end of the bed. Ted was wearing goggles not dissimilar to those donned by our vicar in my drawings. Ted was ready, prepared. There on my desk were my drawings and scrapbooks, these latter yoinked from the Worlds End stationery cupboard. The papers were being tickled by fingers of wind that must have snuck in via the tiny fractures in my window frame. There was wind as well as rain now. The sun struggled on insipidly. The wind was fiercer than anything. I would wear my earmuffs and I would wear them from the moment I got out of bed and dressed.

When I went downstairs St. John wasn't up yet — he wasn't down yet — but my mom had already gone out to work. I could tell because of the small amendments she had left in the rooms she'd passed through on her way out. Her small alterations were spatial kisses. The way she drew the curtains left a smear in the room same as the mark left on my cheek by her lipstick. I clocked the time on my oscarfizzog (after getting over the initial disappointment, I'd started carrying this around with me always) tightened the plastic band of my earmuffs, thought of Indy as I scoffed my cereal. Indy was the only person I had told about the plans me and St. John had been concocting.

"Indy. Hey, Indy."

Idiotically, I had decided to talk to Indy during our weekly Worlds End assembly. To begin with she'd completely ignored me. She had the whole world in her hands, because that was the song we were singing in this assembly and Indy always sang the songs carefully, with a slight lisp. Indy wore a steel bracelet on her right wrist.

"Indy."

Indy — I've already said this — Indy was called Indy after the Last Crusader. Indiana Jones as in the Ark and everything. Indy was also the proud owner of a computer game based on the Indiana Jones movies. We played it when I went round to her house, which was exactly like my house except for the carpets: whereas we had lino, Indy's house had carpets. I was freshly astonished every time I went round there by the carpets and because Indy's mom served stripy ice cream for pudding, something my mom never did.

"INDY."

She rested her eyes, stilled her tongue, and took then took hold of my hand gently. We were too old to hold hands like this, but I decided to let her keep holding if it meant she was going to listen to me.

"I'm going to bury it, with St. John."

Indy relaxed her grip a bit. Her thumbnail was overgrown, I noticed.

"St. John."

She wasn't asking me a question. Indy had repeated St. John's name as if it was a prophecy, or a revelation.

"Yeah, my dad."

She squeezed my hand but didn't look at me.

"But what are you burying, Rita?"

I couldn't believe it.

"Indy. Don't be stupid."

The girl sitting behind me stuck her knee into my thigh-flesh. It hurt but I didn't show it. The Tis'er who played the piano in our assemblies had a tattoo on her upper arm. It skidded out from under her blouse whenever she reached for the really low keys. I had never thought to wonder what the tattoo was a tattoo of. It was a tattoo. That was all. That was enough.

I huffed.

"I'm not burying anything."

Indy looked at me and smiled. I had never before seen her do anything dramatic.

Even though the piano had stopped playing and the Head Tis'er was now saying something, something important probably, Indy started singing at the top of her voice. Everybody turned to look at us.

Indy was singing the K I S S I N G song about me.

"First comes love,
then comes marriage,
then comes a babba
in a perambulator.

That's not it!
That's not all!
The babba's drinking alcohol!

That's not it!
That's not all!
The babba's doing a hula-hula dance!"

Then Indy just stood up. She stood up in a sea of cross-legged y6ers, y5ers, y4ers, and y3ers, turned, and waded through all the rows towards the door at the back of the Worlds End hall. The whole school swiveled their necks to watch her. The few rows that were behind us parted for her as if automatically. The Tis'ers stayed gummed to their seats, stunned. If you wanted to leave Assembly you had to have a really good reason. I didn't know how to go after her. Indy was always being teased, always being shoved about and pushed out from under the canopies, always being told no one would ever want to snog her when the aristotle stopped on her. All I ever did about it was tease her for crying about it. In y6 I cut my hair short, like a boy's. I didn't want to go to school anymore.

That was the last time I had seen Indy in two weeks.

Today was the second Tuesday in a row that I should have been in school but wasn't.

In the days before the excursion, the first days of my absenteeism, my mom forbade me to watch any telly. If I wouldn't go to school, then I couldn't watch my favourite programmes. So I swapped the soft sizzle of the screen for the cold flat panes of our aluminium-framed windows and crossed my fingers behind my coccyx[1] for something worth watching.

---

[1] In the absence of televised entertainment, a loss that was quite traumatic for a (sort-of) only mizzerling, I discovered in the lowest rung of our kitchen bookshelves a Family Health Encyclopedia. It sat next to the book about buildings that St. John recommended when I said what the topic of my project was. Between the entries for 'FARSIGHTEDNESS' and 'NOSEBLEEDS' I inserted a drawing of The Obsolisk and left it there for safe-keeping.

To begin with nothing happened. B24 did as B24 always did. The road outside the window responded with nothing more than an embarrassed stutter. Their bodies condensed, as concise as mine was but simultaneously crinkled in a way that made me queasy, old women passed by our drive dragging tartan bags on wheels behind them. It was only on the third day (but it could easily have been the fourth, or the second) that something new happened, and even then the newness was already old, scuffed, bedraggled. The newness was in the combination.

It was nothing, but in that way that things are to a y6er like Rita, it was everything.

The rag and bone man jangled past in his trap, and our cat, a tabby stray one of the twins had insisted on us adopting, even though both twins were allergic to cats and even though my mom, to whom it inevitably fell to look after it, couldn't bare to touch anything furry — our cat murdered a mouse. I was the one who saw it drop the cadaver on the doormat. The cat had a bloody mouth and scraps of mousemeat between its fangs. It was a gift, St. John said, or at least that was how we should try and think of it, but my mom's mangled scream didn't believe him. The mouse's fur lay scattered around its poor torn body, which the cat had deposited next to our two aristotles of milk and one of orange juice. It occurred to me the cadaver could have been Watt were he not already a goner. I announced as much during pudding at tea that same evening. St. John cooly asked for more blancmange then, when he saw the state of my mom's fizzog, helped himself to a shivering spoonful. It was exactly at that point that the rag and bone melody droned in through our window.

"A-nee-rah-boh. Ah-neeee-rah-boer."

I listened until the syllabling grew loud and immediate.

"AHHH-NEEE-RAHHHH-BOOERR."
"AHHH-NEEE-RAHHH-BOOER."

The rag and bone man's language was as battered, as trashed and as knackered, as the scrap tossed in his cart. His words were as mauled as a mouse's cadaver, but his song was not broken. It was a treacle not of words but of their substance. It wasn't a totally alien sound, the rag and bone man's melody: I had seen him pass by our house once before, and I knew, because my mom said so, that he passed by regularly during school hours, even if I wasn't there to see so. But it was only now that I understood him. The fragments that crashed from his throat were something I now understood. His words were unintelligible only because they were the opposite — only because they were so commonplace. The rag and bone man had sung his moan so many times that the words had worn away, weeped into each other, become blood brothers. At Worlds End our Tis'ers never let us become blood brothers. They had tolerated me threading my finger with the needle for as long as it remained bloodless.

I had never seen anyone on our road open their door to the rag and bone man and deliver their scraps up to him. I wasn't sure what constituted rags and scrap iron, without even getting started on the bones stuff. But I knew I had never seen anyone agree to give away what they did not want anymore. I had never seen anyone agree to give the rag and bone man their bones, their scrap, the crap they had accumulated and no longer knew what to do with. I thought I would give it a go: I thought I'd try to sing back to him. I started warbling. Instead of whatever it was the rag and bone sang, I sang a variation of a sentence I had heard on one of the TV programmes the twins watched. Like Indy before me, I sang, louder and louder.

"Stop it, Rita."

I stopped singing.

"Stop it, bitch," I said.

St. John went on with his blancmange in silence. I concentrated hard on my hatred for a few seconds, then left the table without asking.

I knelt against the window as if it was a pew and I was praying. In our church that had once been a swimming pool, there were no pews.

"Rita."

"*What?*"

"Rita!"

I didn't bother turning around. The rag and bone man's legs were dangling from the front of his four-wheeled trap. His body softly shimmied as the horse he was sitting behind clopped along. I had never ridden or been driven by a horse, and the bob and wobble of the contraption caused a giddiness in my stomach, so I thought. I never was sure how things were caused. In terms of the murmurs I heard coming from inside me, I accepted there was a connection between the food I put in my mouth, or refused to, and the rumblings in my belly, but my belly also ached and pained when I was nervous, or when I had done too much running. It was not only when I was hungry that my stomach hurt me.

The rag and bone man's contraption caught a curb. His elbow jerked upwards.

St. John later told me that the rag and bone man travelled along all roads, even the A4400.

"I don't understand what's got into her."

"..."

"I don't understand what's got into her at *all*."

The rag and bone man's neck was knotted with a handkerchief. On his head was a worn leather cap. He tugged at it a couple of times as he passed. Holding my breath in the same way I did whenever our car went through a tunnel, I watched the trap gradually eradicate each of the letters of our road sign. Then, one by one, as dung pellets simultaneously popped from the horse's lolloping bum, the characters reappeared at the trap's nether end:

ESOLCONIZNAM

St. John and my mom were talking to each other as if I wasn't there.

Was I there?

"She's refusing to go to school. She's not even pretending to be ill anymore."

"She had a fever."

"She didn't."

"I tested her with the thermometer."

"What thermometer? We don't have a thermometer. Where did you get a thermometer from?"

I thought I'd better shove my way back into the world.

"St. John?"

I climbed back into my chair.

"Rita."

He was still looking at my mom even though it was my name that he had spoken. I had nothing to say, so I plucked a question from thin air.

"Does the rag and bone man have a name?"

"He's the rag and bone man."

I paused. I was wearing the striped shirt I usually wore to school. It had my name-tag sewed into the collar.

"So he doesn't have a name?"

"The rag and bone man is his name."

"Is that what his family calls him?"

"Probably."

That was my mom. She stood up and started sweeping the crumbs from the table. I sat myself back in my seat and gripped the table with splayed fingers.

"I wish I was the rag and bone man. I'd keep him company."

"Rita."

"*What?*"

"Don't be ridiculous."

"I'm not."

St. John smiled indecipherably. His teeth were good on the top row, bad on the bottom. Two were missing. He was wearing his favourite pink sweatsuit, the one my mom hated.

"You mean you wish you were a rag and bone man. Then you could keep him company."

"No. I wish I was *the* rag and bone man."

St. John shoveled me a scowl. I ignored it. I knew what I was talking about, so continued.

"The rag and bone man is like Father Christmas. Father Christmas brings new things. The rag and bone man takes them away when they turn into rubbish. There's only one Father Christmas. How can there be more than one rag and bone man?"

"Shall we give you to the rag and bone man?"

That was my mom. It hurt me.

I had wanted to hurt her.

"That's the Child Snatcher's job, stupid."

St. John's smile soured.

"Rita."

"Soz."

"Rita."

"I'm *sorry*."

I really was. Her pleated skirt unfolded and refolded as she moved, slowly, in giraffe time, across the eating space and into the kitchen. The giraffe had been my gran's favourite animal: my mom kept a wooden model of one on top of the bookshelves that contained the cookery books and, on the bottom rung, our Family Health Encyclopedia. Too tall to be positioned beneath it, the bookshelves were positioned to the right of the hatch, the gap between the eating space and the space my mom was in, i.e. the kitchen. The bookshelves were notched and crabby and spat splinters into the palms of your hands. St. John had some books in them too, but barely read them. He watched TV in the living room, eating cashews and raw apples even after my mom had cooked an apple crumble, even after we'd eaten baked potatoes.

I wanted to get up and go to her, but didn't. The rag and bone man's song was as far gone as the mouse the cat killed. I did my best to remember that my mom was not the cat's mom.

"What do you want me to do, Rita?"

I wasn't a giraffe. I was a dead Watt, buried beneath a tiny pebble.

"..."

"Why won't you go to school?"

"I'm on strike."

St. John was staring through the window in the direction of the road sign. His cheeks flushed, and a bend crept back into his lips. He made me an offering.

"Industrial action?"

I wasn't sure whether or not to go with this. After a few moments of deliberation, I decided to go with it.

"Yeah, industrious action."

"No, its opposite."

"What?"

"This isn't helpful, St. John."

I hammered my spoon on the table. It made a metallic crack that had no echo.

"*Rita!*"

"We're going on a trip. I'm taking her on trip."

'Trip' was a word that made me think of the girl falling over in the playground. I laughed.

"What?"

"An excursion."

"*Where?*"

"Well, I thought I could take her with me to the boxing."

In the kitchen my mom was slopping blancmange into the dustbin. The back of her head was a crowd of curls and inside the curls were two hovering earrings. The earrings swung when St. John spoke. Then she looked at us. Her eyes had an intensity again: they were not the opposite of blancmange, but they were more difficult to get into. I rubbed my bare toes against the lino.

"You're not going to the boxing, Rita."

"Why not? There's a match this weekend."

Indy had a picture of a boxing match that her parents wouldn't allow her to pin up on her bedroom wall. St. John was in the picture, stood in the centre of the ring, his hair oily, a hairy hand pointing a microphone to the bloody mouth of the champion. St. John also had a show on the local radio station. That was why his working hours were haphazard. That was why he wasn't there when we gave Watt his burial.

I still said nothing.

In the United States of America, they called gobstoppers *jawbreakers*. Some people believed that *trash* was as American word, but where we lived we knew better. To say *knackered* was to swear, and to get a swipe on your thigh from a fly swat.

In B24, boxing matches were held in the cinema-turned-bingo hall.

"I thought you were going with the twins."

The twins weren't present in the recurring dream I had of their mom, but it was possible, I realised, that their features were present in hers, their mom's, that her fizzog was a combination of theirs plus something else. It was as if the twins themselves had given birth to the version of their mom that I carried inside me. They were either my half-twin-brothers or my twin-half-brothers. They were nothing to do with my mom. They had not been inside her as I had. They were the only thing I ever saw that stood for, or represented, or whatever, St. John's past wife. This meant that the twins were younger than St. John but at the same time they were St.

John's shadow. They were young ghosts of St. John's past, I mean.

St. John had gone all purple.

"What's wrong with that? What have you got against the twins? They're just children."

"They're your children."

Because I thought it might please everyone, I piped up that the twins were my brothers.

St. John ignored me.

"They're my children. Fine. What about you? What if you hadn't lost that baby?"

To get to where the twins lived you had to get across the A4400. They lived not in a house but in a tower block. The twins were non-identical, a characteristic I automatically associated with my own strabismal eyeballs. They called where they lived the Froggery.

"We don't live in *a* froggery, stupid. We live in *the* Froggery."

Come to think of it, it had been a long time since I had waited for St. John while St. John went to see them.

St. John was silent. He was waiting for my mom to say something, but she said nothing. I wiggled in my seat a bit.

"Please can I leave the table?"

It was my mom who nodded, eventually.

St. John never did take me to the boxing. But he didn't make me go back to school for a few weeks, and he did take me on an excursion.

The wind, the day we went, was blowing the rain around ferociously. It blew things up into me: a crisp packet, a dead piss-a-bed. It was annoying. I was glad of my earmuffs. I was impatient to get where we were going: my legs kicked as quick as they could, but whereas St. John was strolling, I was practically full tilt. I bent my head against the wind. St. John didn't seem to be affected. I straggled him. I wanted to go faster, but I was at the same time anxious not to drop the time bomb, the time capsule that St. John had told me to turn my y6 school project into.

"Why the earmuffs?"

St. John was wearing a t-shirt and a bobble hat. So what was wrong with me wearing earmuffs?

"Dad?"

I had to shout after him. The wind shoved the words straight back down my throat, as if I really was eating them.

"Daaad? Hey, Dad!"

He slowed almost to a standstill but kept on stepping forwards. To his left, though he did not stop to look at it, was the lamp-post everybody on our road used as a noticeboard, where people Sellotaped an advertisement for a second-hand piano or, as there was now, a lost cat. The ads usually consisted of a piece of paper with the person's telephone number printed in vertical strips at the bottom. Often these would have been partly cut into by the advertiser, so that you could tear the number off and take it away with you. In the wind these strips bristled. To St. John's right was a low brick wall and, sat smugly on it, a cat, possibly the one from the ad.

The cat purred. St. John stroked it.

"Well?"

"*Well.*"

I wanted to know what was wrong with my mom.

"What's wrong with mom?"

"That's what she keeps asking about you, Rita."

I said nothing. St. John appeared to be gazing at the point where the road shrank to nothing, then turned a bend.

"How's that time machine of yours doing?"

It was just like St. John to change the subject in a way that made you feel he had not changed the subject.

"It's not a time machine. It's a time *capsule*, like you said."

But St. John just blinked at me.

It was an hour and a half, more, maybe, until we next stopped. St. John walked. I lurched. He took no notice of the involuntary burps I kept coughing up. There was a strange pain in my stomach too. But I didn't want to let St. John go off ahead of me. I fell over twice. The first time I grazed my knee slightly. The second time I caught myself awkwardly and got a blood-blister on the palm of my hand. I knew the worst thing I could do would be to pop it. I called out to St. John that I had it. He came and studied it in silence, dusted off the scum that had encrusted it.

We went round in circles. We went along cul-de-sacs, across the wasteland, past the twins' tower block, down manholes, through a skip someone had parked outside their house and dumped all their old furniture in along with a toiletbowl, under The Obsolisk then over the edge of it, past the bingo hall with its oscarfizzog like the one in my pocket, along the cold shoulder of the A4400 with all the cars screaming past us in the opposite direction and above us, hanging like head-choppers, signs saying NORTH and SOUTH in white letters against a blue background. We walked for a time that seemed endless through space that seemed edgeless. Either edgeless or nothing but edge. We walked along the line of the horizon, scrappy as it was with occasional tower blocks like the ones the twins lived in with their mom. We walked the line of the horizon as if it was a tightrope. I got cold and hungry and to top it off we walked past a sign pointing the way to a chocolate faktoroi. We walked past some houses that looked like cottages and when we did St. John said we would soon be walking through the middle of everything. But by that point I had got fed up with stuff. I wanted my mom. I wanted her badly.

The sun made slack attempts to break a ray through the rain-bashed heavens. The blister in the palm my hand was difficult not to fiddle with.

"Dad. Where are we *going*?"

I mustered the courage for this three times.

"Dad, what's wrong with mom?"

St. John didn't answer. In the distance, beyond St. John, I saw the mouth of the same tunnel I held my breath

in whenever we drove through it. We were a long way from
from Worlds End and our church which was once a swimming
pool. We were a long way from everything. Or else we were as
St. John said we were: in the middle of everything. Even then
— even then it took me yonks to choose the burial site.